Financial
DISCIPLESHIP
FOR
Families

Financial DISCIPLESHIP FOR Families

Intentionally Raising
Faithful Children

BRIAN C. HOLTZ

FOREWORD BY ROB WEST

A FINANCIAL DISCIPLESHIP MINISTRY™

© 2023 by Brian C. Holtz and Compass-finances God's way Inc. All rights reserved.

Published by Compass-finances God's way, Inc.

Designed by Jonathan Lewis of Jonlin Creative

Edited by Steve Gardner

ISBN: 979-8-9876968-3-5

All Scripture quotations, unless otherwise indicated, are taken from the Holy Bible, New International Version®, NIV®. Copyright ©1973, 1978, 1984, 2011 by Biblica, Inc.™ Used by permission of Zondervan. All rights reserved worldwide. www.zondervan.com The "NIV" and "New International Version" are trademarks registered in the United States Patent and Trademark Office by Biblica, Inc.™

Scripture quotations identified as (ESV) are from The ESV® Bible (The Holy Bible, English Standard Version®), copyright © 2001 by Crossway, a publishing ministry of Good News Publishers. Used by permission. All rights reserved.

Scripture quotations taken from the (NASB®) New American Standard Bible®, Copyright © 1960, 1971, 1977, 1995, 2020 by The Lockman Foundation. Used by permission. All rights reserved. lockman.org

Scripture quotations marked (NLT) are taken from the Holy Bible, New Living Translation, copyright ©1996, 2004, 2015 by Tyndale House Foundation. Used by permission of Tyndale House Publishers, Carol Stream, Illinois 60188. All rights reserved.

Dedication

To the Father for your amazing and unending love.

To the Son for your unmerited and limitless grace.

To the Spirit for your overwhelming and persistent counsel.

To Erica for your faithful love and support of all that I do.

To Weston, Barrett, Rowan, and Eden for your patience and understanding as I fumble through learning to be a better father.

To my Compass teammates for your passion for God's word and financial principles which encourage and challenge me.

To our financial supporters for your faithful obedience to God's calling to support His ministry.

Contents

Foreword **ROB WEST**	ix
PART 1: LAYING THE FOUNDATION	**13**
Chapter 1: Introduction	15
Chapter 2: The Foundation of Marriage	27
Chapter 3: The Biblical Role of Parents	37
PART 2: A SIMPLE APPROACH TO PARENTING	**51**
Chapter 4: MVP Parenting	53
Chapter 5: Modeling	65
Chapter 6: Verbal Instruction	73
Chapter 7: Practical Opportunities	81
PART 3: FINANCIAL DISCIPLESHIP IN OUR PARENTING	**89**
Chapter 8: Financial Discipleship	91
Chapter 9: Ownership	105
Chapter 10: Surrender	117
Chapter 11: Choice	139
Chapter 12: Multiplication	159
Chapter 13: Eternal Focus	171
PART 4: FINISHING TOUCHES	**183**
Chapter 14: Outside Influences	185
Chapter 15: MVP Everything	203
Chapter 16: Finishing Well	217
About the Author	233
Endnotes	235

Foreword

How often, as parents, do we wish our children were born with instruction manuals? We love our kids, and want the best for them, but so often, we find ourselves repeating the mistakes of the past – either ours or our own parents'. This is especially true when it comes to teaching our kids how to handle money and possessions. If managing money isn't your strong suit, or if you've made some financial mis-steps in your life, you might even feel like you're not qualified to teach your children in this area. Let me reassure you that you are, in fact, uniquely qualified, and *Financial Discipleship for Families* is an excellent tool to help along the way.

As Christian parents, we have the responsibility and privilege of discipling our children as they grow, teaching them to love and follow Christ. Part of that calling involves leading them into a biblical understanding of stewardship. Stewardship happens when we recognize that "the earth is the Lord's, and everything in it." (Psalm 24:1) Everything we own, earn, and desire belongs to God, and we are the managers of the resources He provides. From a biblical perspective, good money management is less about teaching the rules than reaching the heart.

Why is our attitude about money and possessions so important? Well, money is like a truth serum – your attitudes and actions regarding material possessions reveal a lot about your spiritual condition. In my 17 years of financial radio ministry, I have become convinced that money, for the Christian, is more a matter of the heart than the pocketbook. In Luke 12:34, Jesus said,

"Where your treasure is, there your heart will be also." So, if we're focused on getting and keeping money, we'll have less room for getting and keeping a relationship with Jesus. The sobering truth is, when "things" occupy our energy and thoughts, God takes second place. This is a dangerous and ultimately untenable mindset for a believer. Jesus himself makes this clear in Luke 16:13: "You cannot serve both God and money," he tells his disciples. Given that truth, we cannot afford to ignore our own attitudes – or our children's – about material things.

Thus, a healthy relationship with God requires a true understanding of our own position regarding money and material possessions. Once you submit to the idea that God owns everything, your perspective on "stuff" changes. You cease being an owner, and all the responsibility of ownership passes into the hands of Almighty God. The transition from "mine" to "His" can be painful, but in the end, there's peace in knowing that God is sovereign.

Children start life with a decidedly self-centered perspective. Watch any group of young children playing, and you're sure to hear that word "mine" fairly often. Left unchecked, the natural selfishness of childhood can become something dreadful in an adult – from an attitude of entitlement, to greed, envy, and self-indulgence. Families that practice biblical stewardship together can break the power of selfish desires, replacing it with virtues of patience, generosity, gratitude, and godly wisdom.

Financial Discipleship for Families walks with you as you submit your marriage, parenting, and finances to the Lordship of Christ. Practical steps and spiritual insights together will make the process a joyful adventure for the entire family. Along the way, you'll strengthen your relationships with each other and the Lord as you develop an eternal perspective on your money and material possessions.

Ultimately, we parents hope to launch young adults who have their financial priorities straight, and who desire to serve the Lord and those around them through biblical, joyful stewardship of their time, talents, and treasure. Our prayer as they leave the fold is that they will "stand firm in the faith, be courageous, be strong, and do everything in love." (1 Corinthians 16:13 – 14)

I am delighted to recommend this clear, family-tested approach to teaching biblical financial principles. Brian Holtz and his wife are in the thick of raising a family of four, so the concepts he shares come from where he's living. If that's where you are, too, then you're in the right place.

Rob West
CEO, Kingdom Advisors
Host, Faith & Finance

PART 1

Laying the Foundation

CHAPTER 1

Introduction

Train up a child in the way he should go.
Even when he is old, he will not depart from it.
PROVERBS 22:6 (ESV)

WHY CHRISTIAN PARENTING?
I know it sounds cheesy (something I won't make a habit of in this book) but being a parent has proven to be an amazing experience.

I still remember when our first child was born, when I held this little human for the first time. It was a little after six in the morning on the fourth of July, 2009. It had stormed all night and the sun was beginning to light up the world through still-cloudy skies. He was born relatively happy and healthy, and Erica was recovering. That was when I got my first chance to hold him. I looked down at that little face and marveled at his amazing potential. Not in the sense that he could be an astronaut if he put his mind to it. In the sense that he was new, unblemished, a blank slate.

Like you, I have been changed by my experiences. One experience at a time, I have gone from who I was to who I am becoming—with varying degrees of awareness at the time. My God-given traits were my starting point, but my experiences had changed me—the way I was raised, the things I was taught, the successes and failures I had, the time I got busted stealing candy from a store, the time a kid I hadn't hung out with in years stood up for me against his new friends.

All my previous experiences, good and bad, had formed who I was at that moment: my personality type, my sense of humor, my profession, and my vocation. One small change at a time, I became someone with unique perspectives and skills, but also limitations.

I can look back and see how God put all these things together for my good, but it certainly wasn't the straightest path, and I often didn't see where I was headed. This little human, on the other hand, had none of that. He had the fresh start I had wanted for a long time. Although he didn't have the wisdom I had accumulated from my stack of experiences, he also wasn't saddled with the baggage. That was my first thought.

My second thought was equally profound but far less inspiring: "Don't mess him up."

As his parent, I now have the responsibility of helping him avoid the worst of life's experiences while embracing the best it has to offer—to become who God has made him to be. I have responsibility for training this new person in the way he should go so that even when he is old he will not depart from it.

In the years since that day, I have been on a proverbial roller coaster of emotions: the joy of seeing him succeed, the sadness of seeing him struggle, the laughter of hearing him tell his first joke, the pride I feel when he shows love and kindness to strangers (and occasionally even his siblings), the frustration of his arguing everything (even when I agree with his stated position), and the anger that comes when he ignores my warnings and leaves a mess for me to clean up. But in all that, my greatest gain from being a parent is the little taste of how God must feel.

He created me for a purpose. He left me instructions to help and His Spirit to guide moment by moment. Sometimes I trust His plan; other times I don't. Sometimes I listen to His voice; other times I insist that my way will work better. Sometimes I reflect His goodness; other times I stand in opposition to it.

On a few occasions, I have done things that I hope bring a smile to His face and have Him turning to the apostle Paul and saying,

"That's my boy!" Other times I am sure He shakes his head and looks forward to the day I figure this stuff out.

Above all else, being a parent has given me incredible insight into the nature of God: His wisdom, His goodness, and His patience toward us, *His* children. And now He gives us as parents the responsibility to train our children well, teaching them good from bad, right from wrong, beneficial from counterproductive. Like His Spirit sent to be our Counselor and Comforter, we have been placed in our unique positions to instruct our children (when they'll listen) and influence them (when they won't).

This book aims to unify and address two core callings of Christian parents. First, as Christians, we are to be faithful followers of Jesus, growing more in His likeness every day in every area of our lives. Second, as parents, we are to be the chief disciplers of our children, training them to follow Jesus as we do.

This book establishes foundational principles for each of these two callings, then unites them for specific application to your money and possessions so that you and your children can glorify God with your finances.

The Best Defense is a Good Offense

Sadly, many parents, including Christian parents, don't *ACTIVELY* parent. We *REACTIVELY* parent on a more or less as-needed basis. But our anchor verse, Proverbs 22:6, says, *"Train up a child in the way he should go . . ."* It does *not* say, "Correct your child when they make a mistake." But in truth, merely correcting mistakes is all that many of us aspire to as parents.

God instructs us to train, an active endeavor meant to prepare the trainee for a specific task. And the expectation is that we will train our children how to think, how to discern, how to make good, godly decisions. Unfortunately, we often opt to just sit back, hoping we can swoop in at just the right moment to convey our wisdom. We expect, in that moment, they will do as we say without hesitation or question.

This approach has a few major flaws. First, it assumes we have control of our children. If you already have children, you've learned that if there is anything we *don't* have, it's control (Can I get an "Amen!").

Maybe you imagine you control your newborn since they are physically unable to do anything without you. Just wait till they turn two. The control you thought you had is nearly gone and they are barely walking. This is where embracing our INFLUENCE comes in. Through my own experiences as a parent, I have seen (and been alarmed by) how little control and how much influence I have over my kids.

Even when I have accurately predicted a fork-in-the-road moment and told them exactly how to handle it, they haven't listened. Without instructing them at all though, they have learned my mannerisms, behaviors, and vocabulary. Although I can't choose or predict what they learn from me, I can't deny that they *are* learning from me. And so the most effective way to help them is not to tell them what to do in the moment, but to teach them ahead of time how to look at and react to certain situations. This is the power of influence. It is the long road for sure, but it is the godly road.

God could have sought to control us, but he chose instead to influence us. His commands are just as descriptive as they are prescriptive. In all of it, He saw value in allowing us to go whichever way we wanted, value in exerting His influence rather than His control. And He alone had the ability to do either. As parents with similar responsibilities, we need to approach our parenting the same way.

The second major flaw of reactive parenting is that it results in us being unprepared for even the fork-in-the-road moments, leading us to respond in ways we would not have preferred. In active parenting, we look forward and consider: What would I want my child to do? How can I guide them in that direction now? How should I respond if they don't follow my guidance?

This gives us the opportunity to think through our possible responses, to seek God's instruction in the Bible, and to listen to His counsel in prayer. It allows us to formulate a plan for how we can best influence our children gradually and even address it directly, should the need arise. It challenges us to compare how our child SHOULD behave with how we, in fact, DO behave.

Reactive parenting, on the other hand, results in emotional confrontations. We end up in a succession of "broccoli battles," which occur when we could have predicted they would refuse to eat the broccoli, but we never planned for how to address it in a productive and Christ-like manner.

When we reactively respond to their resistance, we generally do it with idle threats like not letting them eat any dinner ever again or not allowing them to go to bed until every piece of broccoli is gone. They have a melt-down (or even worse, act like they don't care), which frustrates us more than it does them. And it just perpetuates the cycle of emotional rather than theological—or even logical—responses.

When we have actively thought through how we could influence and address our children's choices, we come up with better, more Spirit-filled responses. We still won't avoid all fork-in-the-road moments, but we will reduce them and make the remainder easier to manage.

And more importantly, if we cannot lead well reactively on the topic of eating vegetables, how will we handle the big issues like drug use, teen pregnancy, and "I'm moving to Tijuana with some friends"?

No amount of active parenting can guarantee that our children won't choose a wrong path, but embracing our influence through active parenting significantly reduces those risks. It creates a path of love for how we move forward from wherever we find ourselves.

There's an even scarier part to this reactive parenting trap. In the absence of our active guidance and instruction, the world fills the gap. When we choose not to actively teach our children how to maneuver the inevitable situations of life, others step in and do it on their terms. The world's influence pours in through friends, powerful media of all kinds, politicians, even educators.

As parents of four energetic and inquisitive kids, Erica and I often have to point out to them that they have us outnumbered. "I know you're only asking us one question per minute, but there are four of you and two of us, so each of us has answered a question every 30 seconds for the last four years."

The world's numerical advantage is even greater. While there are only two of us to parent our four kids, there are millions of YouTubers, influencers, TV show characters, sports heroes, musicians, friends, marketing execs, etc. We can try the parenting whack-a-mole game where we just shut off every bad influence on our children, but we don't stand a chance of keeping up. Every bad influence we squash can be replaced by seven others. Jesus makes this point in Luke 11:24-26.

> *"When an impure spirit comes out of a person, it goes through arid places seeking rest and does not find it. Then it says, 'I will return to the house I left.' When it arrives, it finds the house swept clean and put in order. Then it goes and takes seven other spirits more wicked than itself, and they go in and live there. And the final condition of that person is worse than the first."*

Although not directly talking about parenting, Jesus is teaching us that it is not good enough to just remove the bad from our lives: we must aggressively replace it with the good. If we sit back and allow the world to raise our kids, we should not be surprised when we find their values and behaviors more closely resembling the world's than our Savior's.

There is, of course, a simple reason most of us choose not to actively parent. It's a lot of work. I know it seems too obvious and a little insulting, but it's the truth. Active parenting requires us to make plans, to engage, to commit, to devote. It requires us to define goals, to build strategies and contingencies. It requires us to be "on-duty" anytime they are, which is always.

It's easier to parent reactively, no doubt about it, but if we are going to live up to our calling as parents, to fulfill the role God created, active parenting is our only choice. The alternative is to put your hope in the luck of the draw.

In the corporate world, we had a saying, "Hope is not a strategy." Your first reaction may be that, theologically speaking, hope *is* a strategy, and really the only one we have. But I beg to differ. Hope is not the theological strategy for salvation: faith is.

I know the difference seems subtle but stay with me here. Consider the difference between these two statements: "I hope Jesus saves me." and, "I have faith that Jesus will save me." Hoping my kids turn out to be Christians while not having a plan to accomplish it is just a wish. But faith, the intentional choice to believe in things we cannot see, is absolutely a strategy, and one worth pursuing.

None of us would say, "I have faith that if I allow the world to parent my kids for me, they will grow to be faithful followers of Christ." We may *hope* that is true, but it is only a wish with no plan. Instead, we must have faith that if we follow God's instructions, He will fulfill His promise of good in our lives and in our children's lives. That's a strategy I can get behind!

Establishing a Baseline

Part of our goal as Christian parents is to establish a baseline for our children that sets them up for success, first spiritually, then emotionally, and finally physically.

I have noticed a funny thing with families (mine and others). What we experience as children establishes our expectations throughout our lives. We all think our families are "normal." But as we spend time with friends' families as kids or perhaps later with college roommates, we quickly learn that not everyone is like us. The things that were "normal" in our upbringing are not "normal" for others. Their traditions are different. Their interactions are different. They don't have the Holtz-family 24-hour refrigerator rule that anything left in the refrigerator past 24 hours is fair game, name written on it or not.

There is another thing you need to know about me before we get too far, so I guess now is as good a time as any to share it: we have chickens. Yep, we're those people. I don't remember why we got them in the first place, but we did, and we still do. This is relevant now because having chickens has created a very strange but illustrative example of how pliable our kids' beliefs and attitudes are when they are young.

My kids think white eggs are weird and inedible. My oldest son was three years old when we first got chickens. They all laid brown eggs. Since then, we have added pink, blue, and green egg layers, but never white. So when we run out of eggs and my wife has to buy them from the store, our kids look in amazement at the carton of perfectly white eggs.

They ooh and aah, but they don't eat them. We can usually sneak them into some baked goods, but if we just fry up an egg, they won't touch it.

Their friends come over and are amazed at the cornucopia of colors in our cartons but our kids don't even flinch. Why? Because that's their baseline. That's their normal. While the other kids have always had white eggs, our kids have never had them. Their friends think our eggs are amazingly weird, and our kids think white eggs are a freak of nature second only to a three-eyed squirrel.

As Christians, we are called to be different. We are called to stand out in a way that's attractive and engages people, drawing them closer to Christ. As parents, we have the opportunity to help our children develop baselines that prepare them to live more Christ-focused and devoted lives than we had.

As you will find throughout the book, the concept of establishing a baseline is foundational to helping them mature into strong followers of Christ. Even if our children choose not to follow our example or counsel, we can help them establish healthier assumptions and perspectives that will result in better outcomes than if we had done nothing but hope.

WHY MONEY?

Money carries incredible power in our society, but that's not new. The Bible has 2,350 verses about money and possessions—not because money is more important than prayer, faith, or love—but because it is so relatable and tempting to us. It's also analogous to anything else we care deeply about.

We all interact with money on a daily basis, and few of us are immune to worries about not having enough, or pride when we have too much. Money is the accepted currency of life on earth in the past, present, and near-term future.

We have all heard that *"The love of money is a root of all kinds of evil"* (1 Timothy 6:10), but why is that true? The short answer (lots more to come in the remaining chapters) is that money allows us to—at least on the surface—replace dependence *on* God with independence *from* God.

God is supposed to be my provider, but if I have enough money I can provide for myself. God is supposed to be my comforter, but with enough money I can surround myself with people who will listen to and encourage me. God is supposed to be my counselor, but with enough money I can hire a professional. God is supposed to be my savior, but with enough money I can numb the brokenness and forget I need saving. On the surface, these seem like drastic leaps, but whether it is a little crack in the dam or a big one, the dam is failing, and it is failing for each of us.

And while society's choice to replace God with money is a very bad thing, it gives Christians a great opportunity. As we said earlier, we are called as children of God to be different. Though we would prefer the world not be saturated in materialism and greed, it gives us a ministry opportunity to stand out in a good way.

As we display contentment rather than materialism, generosity rather than greed, and joy rather than judgment, the world will naturally wonder what's going on with us crazy Christians. They may even wonder how they can join in. How can we care so much about people and so little about money, and how can they have that kind of heart? Why aren't we worried about (fill in the blank with the crisis of the week), and how can they have that kind of peace in their lives? These questions have led people to Jesus for 2,000 years, and the same questions will lead our children to Him as well.

This book is about helping your family, led by you, to have a healthier relationship with God through a healthier relationship with money. It is not meant to get you out of debt, save for college, build wealth, or leave an inheritance. Those things may happen too, but they aren't what this is about. In many ways, you will find this book about money to not really be first and foremost about money. It is about your relationship with God through the use of money, how you can help your children develop a healthier relationship with God through their use of money, and how those same biblical financial principles can be applied to every area of your life.

WHY ME AND WHY YOU?

Now we come to the brass tacks. Why did I—as opposed to someone else—write this book, and why should you read it—as opposed to the other books you could be reading? In short, because I am a fairly normal guy who loves the Lord and wants my kids to love the Lord. I've messed up (and continue to mess up) in my efforts to help them, and for a long time I've ignored the impact money and my parenting has had on my family's spiritual well-being.

I grew up just south of Chicago in a family that went to church but pretty much left God there between Sundays. I walked away from God as a teenager. I was a decent but not great kid in high school. I went to college to earn a degree I don't really use. I turned back to God, got married to a wife way out of my league, and had a kid. Got deployed for a year while falling into financial ruin (thank you, Great Recession). We dug out of the pit by applying secular financial principles but soon found ourselves headed back toward the same pit. We had another kid. I discovered the Bible had quite a few things to say about money and started studying and applying the Bible's teachings. We had another kid. And another kid. And yes, I understand what's causing all the kids.

I'm probably a lot like you in many of these respects. Maybe you can't check every box on my list, but you probably have more than a few. Probably unlike you, though, I have earnestly studied God's word and what it says about money and possessions in a way most would think is insane. After a relatively successful 15-year corporate career, I was called into full-time ministry with Compass-finances God's way. I am committed to seeing people set free from the burdens of materialism and greed so that they may know Christ more intimately, be free to serve Him, and help fund the Great Commission.

I write this book not as an expert in the field of Christian parenting. Those books have their place. Sage advice from people who have successfully climbed the mountain and share their unique perspectives is irreplaceable in the growth of Christians—on this topic or any other. But this isn't that book.

I'm more like the guy a few turns ahead on the trail. The one who lets you know to watch out for the bear scat on the left because it's still fresh. The size 10 shoe print will prove it. I don't write this book as a General with all the answers. I write it as a fellow soldier in the trenches with you whose only advantage is a head start.

Unlike the wise sage who has successfully completed their parenting, I'm still in the battle. Should you ever happen to meet me, you will find me remarkably unremarkable. Should you ever meet my children, you will find them to be perfectly imperfect. Despite having a dad who literally wrote the book on helping kids develop a God-glorifying relationship with money, they still struggle with materialism and greed, each with their own unique tendencies and inclinations. They have no doubt learned some, if not most, from me. But what I lack in expertise in the area of Christian parenting, I make up for in commitment to influencing my kids in the direction of Christ, especially in the area of money and possessions, and to helping others do the same.

Throughout this book, I will teach in principles, explain with examples, and always ground my thoughts and ideas in Scripture. None of the ideas I share will work for all your kids. None of them even work for all *MY* kids. But, as we noted earlier in this chapter, we must do something, even if it's not perfect.

Use my ideas if they fit, adapt them where you prefer, throw them out if you must, but don't do nothing. Like it or not, intentionally or unintentionally, actively or reactively, we are training our children. If we are going to be godly parents training godly children, we must roll up our sleeves, put on our tall boots, and get to the work of intentionally parenting our children in the area of money and possessions.

The alternative is equal parts easy and unacceptable. God has given each one of us the responsibility and gift of our children. Not only to make more little Jesus-followers, but also to refine us in the fire of parenthood so that we ourselves may be more like His Son every day.

So, let's get to work.

Three Biggest Takeaways from this Chapter - This is my favorite way of "digesting" what I've read. Go back and reread the things you underlined, highlighted, or noted. Then, try to boil it all down to the three biggest "takeaways." It's also a great platform for discussion with your spouse or small group.

1)

2)

3)

CHAPTER 2

The Foundation of Marriage

> *That is why a man leaves his father and mother and is united to his wife, and they become one flesh.*
>
> GENESIS 2:24

At first glance, it may seem odd that the second chapter in a book about teaching children godly financial principles would be about marriage, but it shouldn't. This chapter will help us better understand what it takes to create a marriage that is healthy for our children. It also prepares us for marriage's implications in raising financial disciples in our homes.

As we read in Genesis, God created everything, and everything was *"good"* except the state of human existence. God looked at His lonely creation without a suitable companion and declared it *"not good"* (Genesis 2:18). God quickly resolves this by taking a part of man and making woman. This results in the second thing that isn't *"good,"* because it's found to be *"very good"* (Genesis 1:31)!

This partnership created by God in reflection of His own triune existence established our need for the opposite sexes and provides the foundation of the family. It was in response to the creation of male and female that *"God blessed them and said to them, 'Be fruitful and increase in number..."* (Genesis 1:28).

We see throughout Scripture that children should be the product of marriage, and that marriage should be until death. We find, however, in our society and even in our churches that marriage is not treated as permanent. Sadly, it's often treated as an emotional commitment, replacing "till death do us part" with "till I think I'd be happier without you."

With only the few extreme exceptions presented in Matthew 5:31-32 and 1 Corinthians 7, Christian marriage should be viewed as much as a commitment to endure as it is to enjoy. Ideally, we will enjoy every moment with our spouse, but we must always fall back on the commitment we made to God and our spouse that even when we don't enjoy it, we will endure it.

It's not romantic, but that's kind of the point. Biblical love is an action, not an emotion. When we promised to love our spouse, we promised to care for them even when it's inconvenient. To be kind to them even when we're mad. To honor them even when we don't want to. And to engage with them even when we would rather check out.

This level of commitment is essential for the proper spiritual, emotional, intellectual, and physical development of our children. That is how God designed it to work best.

If you are a single parent, I have good news, bad news, and more good news. The first good news is that the bad news is not a surprise to you. You figured it out a long time ago and are living it every day of your life. And that bad news is, of course, that you've got to step in as both parents.

For the time that you have your kids, you are both mom and dad. I know you weren't made to be both, and it's more than double the work, but here we are. Every time Erica is sick and I have to do everything, I'm reminded of what single parents do every day and what an impossible task it is. Even if you can't do everything all the time, do what you can as often as you can.

Whether or not your children acknowledge it, your commitment to them is making a profound impact on the way they see the world. In ways they may never understand or communicate, they are learning what Christlike love and sacrifice is: a person giving their life so that others can live.

The second good news is that it is much easier to get alignment on how to handle many of the difficult decisions parents have to make. We will talk more about managing outside influences later, but alignment happens *inside* your home. Once you've discerned God's will in a matter, you have instant alignment. No second person to convince. There are dangers to this, but benefits as well.

I'll also add that you should use the guidance in this book regarding marriage, parenting, and finances as selection criteria if you consider bringing a new parent into your home (and your kids' lives). You'll want someone who shares your faith, your commitment to applying biblical principles and actively parenting your children. Someone who desperately wants to see them come to faith in Christ and follow godly financial principles. You and your kids need and deserve that. Accept nothing less.

COMMITMENT

Timothy Keller, in his book *The Meaning of Marriage*,[1] points out that we marry with an eagerness to learn more of the good things about our partner. But we are actually set up for the very opposite. In our dating experience, we are exposed to a small part of who they really are, the parts that happen to come up, filtered by what they want to show.

Very few of us roll out of bed and head out to our first date unshowered and dressed in whatever we happen to be wearing. We want to make a good impression and put our best foot forward. We get cleaned up, pick out the clothes that will most impress our date, and make sure every hair is in its proper place. We hold our tongue when we might otherwise speak up. We're extra polite to the waiter when he messes up our order.

But once we're married, we no longer feel the need to put on that image. Even if we did, it would be logistically impossible. Our spouse sees both the best and worst of us. They see our pure motives as we respond in unforced kindness and they see when we instinctively snap back after we've had a bad day.

This is why marriage vows include the good and the bad. For better and for worse. In sickness and in health. For richer and for poorer. Till death do us part. This is the commitment required for marriage because we get both good and bad in our shared life. As R. Kent Hughes[2] puts it, "Marriage will reveal something about your wife that you already know about yourself—that she is a sinner." And your spouse can say the same about you! While it's scary that we committed to love things we didn't know and could never have predicted, there's tremendous freedom in knowing that commitment covers all.

With only those few extreme biblical exceptions, when we commit to marriage, we commit for life. Much like our walk with Christ, this can be either an advantage or something we take advantage of. When we accept eternal forgiveness, we can either use it as our unlimited get-out-of-jail-free card or as a reason to be better. We can either keep on sinning, knowing that we're forgiven, or we can be motived by that forgiveness to *"Go now and leave your life of sin"* (John 8:11).

In the same way, the unconditional commitment of our spouse can give us either a reason to relax or a reason to step up. I no longer need to impress Erica, but it's even more meaningful to her that I still want to. She no longer needs to rub my neck when I sleep funny, so it means even more that she still does. Our commitment can be either an excuse to be lax, or a reason to be better. As Hughes later points out, through it all we are challenged to ask ourselves whether our spouse is being made more like Christ because of our marriage. That must be our goal.

Finances are one of the most common reasons for divorce in the United States (second only to infidelity), and I'd argue that they are a contributing factor to many of the other reasons offered (lack of communication, arguing, unrealistic expectations, etc.). Whether it's because there's a disagreement over how to handle finances, arguments because finances haven't been handled well, or stress because there doesn't seem to be enough, finances often drive people apart.

Although many of our worst traits are exposed by how we handle money, how we handle it can also help us build greater trust and confidence in our future together. Like all other issues, when you have a dispute about money and are able to work through it, the result is a greater confidence that your spouse is really in this "till death do us part." She didn't bail because you didn't agree. He didn't leave because you made a mistake. You were able to talk about things you don't want to talk about and stay committed to your life together. These interactions build a strong foundation one brick at a time.

COMMON VISION

Do you ever think about what it means for something to be "good"? We throw the term around but rarely think about what it really means. With C. S. Lewis, I believe when we say something is "good," what we mean is that it fulfills its purpose.

I drive a fifteen year old pickup truck. It has 230,000 miles on it and squeaks like it runs on hamsters. Is it a "good" vehicle? Well, it depends. When I want to take all my kids somewhere, it's not "good," because I can only take three passengers. When I just need to get to and from work, it is "very good," because it always starts.

If I ask you to go outside and find a "good" rock, what kind of rock do I want you to pick up? Well, it depends. If I need a paperweight, a small round rock would be good. If I need a doorstop, a bigger rock will be better. And if I want to show off my amazing rock-skipping skills, a flat rock will be needed (along with a miracle). "Good" depends on purpose.

This is an issue we often run into in life, including in marriage and family. In my corporate life, my specialty was stepping into chaotic situations and bringing stability. I'm naturally gifted at seeing and understanding patterns (numbers, behaviors, clouds, doesn't matter what). This helped me to see through the noise of the situation and figure out what was really going on.

But first I needed to know the goal. What are we trying to accomplish? What are the keys to success? How is it supposed to work? Once I knew the purpose of the processes, I could quickly see where things were going well and not so well.

The same goes for parenting. To be successful at raising our children, we need to determine what "successful" means.

As Christians, we should recognize that our purpose is to bring glory to God (Revelation 4:11, Psalm 115:1, Matthew 5:16, 1 Corinthians 6:20, 1 Corinthians 10:31, and many others). In order for us to live a "good" life, the things we do and say must accomplish that purpose. Our marriages must accomplish that purpose. Our parenting must accomplish that purpose. Our jobs and hobbies must accomplish that purpose. And our use of money and possessions must accomplish that purpose.

One of the most challenging parts of "two becoming one" is that we start out very different. It's often like welding iron to concrete (for those who don't know about welding, you can't weld to concrete because it's not metal). We have different "baselines," different core assumptions about life, and different goals for life. Before we can successfully influence our children toward where we want them to go, we need to get alignment on where it is we want them to go.

Here are a few questions to consider and discuss that will help you:

1. What is the purpose of our family?
2. What Bible verses or passages best illustrate, summarize, or emphasize that purpose?
3. What are the five greatest things we want for our child(ren) in their life (first should be salvation)?
4. What can we do to help influence them toward the things we want for them?

Do you see what I'm getting at here with the Common Vision thing? If we are going to get alignment on the fourth question, we need to get alignment on the first one. If I think we're headed to Maine and Erica thinks we're headed for Oregon, our kids won't have a clue where to go.

Our family is still working through some of this, but here's what we know for sure:

- We want our kids to accept salvation through Jesus.

- We want our kids to live in a manner that shows the love of Christ to the world.
- We want our kids to use finances to bring glory to God.
- If our kids grow up to be Spirit-filled followers of Jesus, Christ-like husbands and wives, and Father-like fathers and mothers, we will have been successful as parents.

When discussions come up—and they do often—we have these ideals to go back to as a point of reference. We may disagree on how to best achieve these shared goals, but we at least know that our goals are the same. We can fall back on and build off of that.

COMMUNICATION

Building on the groundwork of a fully committed relationship and the need for common vision, we'll now turn to the importance of communication in our marriages, especially about finances.

For some reason, talking about finances is awkward. I think it's because it exposes our differing baselines, experiences, and perspectives, forcing us to confront these underlying differences. It seems like something that shouldn't matter but very much does. We think that because the love of money is a root of all kinds of evil, we should just avoid the topic and pretend it isn't there. This is very unfortunate. Like most other revealing topics, the best treatment is to bring them to light rather than hide them (or *from* them), especially in the context of a "till death do us part" marriage.

At Compass-finances God's way, we encourage people to go on what we call Money Dates. These are just couples setting aside time to talk about finances on a regular basis. You can go out to eat or just stay at home. Nothing formal or awkward needed. Discuss things like:

- What were your experiences with money growing up?
- What are our financial goals?
- What sort of things do we want to give to?
- How expensive of a thing are you okay with me buying without your input?
- How do we want to handle college tuition?

- When do we want to retire and what will we do?

Each of these questions, basic as they may be, lead to much deeper, soul-searching questions about who we are, how we got that way, what we value, who we want to be, and how we should get there. They start out as each individual telling their own story, but gradually the two stories become one. That common vision we talked about earlier is formed through communication made possible by a committed, trusting relationship of marriage.

Just as importantly, these scheduled conversations break the ice for the more challenging conversations like:

- The car broke down again. Now what?
- I just lost my job. What are we going to do?
- My brother wants to borrow money again. What do you think?

Proverbs 15:22 tells us, *"Plans fail for lack of counsel, but with many advisors they succeed."* It is a good practice to run any big decision past people whose values align with ours and whose perspectives we trust.

The first of these advisors, in nearly all matters, should be our spouse. Howard Dayton, founder of Compass-finances God's way, openly shares the value he received from talking about financial decisions with his now-late wife, Bev, who had no background in finance whatsoever. He points out that seeking our spouse's counsel first taps into their unique gifts, experiences, and perspectives. It creates shared successes and failures (avoiding one person taking all the credit or blame), prepares both spouses for the future, and, most importantly, honors them as an essential part of the marriage.

When two became one, we willingly surrendered our independence and must now fulfill that commitment by including our spouse in every part of our life.

As I write this, I'm just now realizing that what I'm advocating for here is having an active marriage as the foundation for our active parenting. By having forward-looking conversations before the need arises, it becomes easier to make healthy and Spirit-filled decisions when under pressure. Too often we try to maintain a reactive marriage, avoiding tough topics until they are no longer avoidable, which makes them even more threatening. By opening the line of communication when the stress is low, we strengthen it for times when the stress is high.

Most of us would rather avoid the confrontations that will likely result from different experiences, perspectives, and ideas. The greater risk, though, is that we don't talk about any of it: low-stress or high, small issue or big. We attempt to execute this shared life of "two become one" separately. But it doesn't work. In marriage and parenting, we become inseparable in a way we can't understand. That's how God made it.

Remember how we used our commitment to endure as a reason to express and share our enjoyment rather than withhold it? We should also use it to take the risk of making the waters a little choppy by talking out our differences—knowing that our spouse has committed to life with us, knowing it will be to the ultimate benefit of our marriage.

WRAPPING UP ON MARRIAGE

While we will all enjoy a healthy marriage more than any alternative, the greatest beneficiaries of a healthy marriage are our children. As they see and hear us engage in tough conversations with love and respect, that becomes their baseline. They learn that money and relationships are gifts from God, intended to be used for His glory and our good. They go to school believing they are safe and loved by parents who are safe and loved by each other. They enter relationships believing that's the norm (though we know too well it isn't) and refusing to accept anything less. They speak and act affectionately toward their spouse and children later in life and don't apologize for it.

I have a personal goal in life that my kids will one day realize how weird our family was—how different from the baseline of their friends. I want them to someday realize that not all parents kiss and hug each other in front of their kids, but they should. I want them to someday realize that not all families pray at dinner and mow lawns for the elderly, but they should. I want them to someday realize that not all families choose to deprioritize vacations so they can help others in need, but they should. I want them completely convinced when they go off to college that unconditional love comes from God, through parents, and be surprised when their friends say that's not how it was for them. I want them to be different and to thank God (and us) for it.

THREE BIGGEST TAKEAWAYS FROM THIS CHAPTER

1)

2)

3)

CHAPTER 3

The Biblical Role of Parents

*Fathers, do not exasperate your children;
instead, bring them up in the training
and instruction of the Lord.*

EPHESIANS 6:4

If you've never noticed it before, pay special attention to the theme of parents and children in the Bible. You don't need to go to any particular section to find it. In fact, you'll have a tough time avoiding it. Whether in passages speaking literally about parents and their children or analogously, it's all over the place. In fact, it's one of the fundamental structures of human existence.

Literally no one exists without biological parents (Jesus only had one, but He *did* have *one*). We all know that contributing biologically to the creation of a child isn't the same as being a "parent." True parenting requires more. To be the "Abba" kind of parent Jesus knew in His Dad, we must embrace the role and its many responsibilities.

Just as we discussed in the last chapter, having the goal of being a "good" parent begs the question, what does it mean to be a "good" parent? Which leads to, what is the purpose of a parent?

I believe the purpose of parents is to create the best environment for their children to grow into faithful Christian adults. I settle on this goal for a few reasons. First, it's God-centered. If our purpose is to bring glory to God, that needs to be the primary goal of our children's lives as well.

Second, it rightly limits our responsibility to "creating an environment." We may not be able to make the proverbial horse take a drink, but we can certainly lead it to water.

Lastly, it puts the ultimate choice on our children as they grow into adults. Each of us is called to *"work out your salvation . . ."* (Philippians 2:12). Accepting Christ's offer of forgiveness is ultimately an individual decision, one our children must make for themselves.

With this goal in mind, the Bible gives us three fundamental categories of parental responsibility: to protect, to provide, and to prepare. These three create a strong platform to discuss how we can help our children grow into faithful followers of Jesus, including with their finances.

PROTECT

As parents, our first calling is to protect our children. This includes physically, emotionally, and spiritually. This call to protect does not imply that fear should be our primary motivation as parents, but Jesus is pretty direct about His position on those who hurt children when He says in Luke 17:2, *"It would better for them to be thrown into the sea with a millstone tied around their neck than to cause one of these little ones to stumble."* Generally, when we think about the minimum requirement of being a parent, this is it. We don't want to make them stumble, and we want to help them navigate around others who might.

When they are newborns, it's not letting them get trampled by the dog or their siblings. As toddlers, it's keeping them from walking into the road and making sure they get the right medicine when they're sick. As grade-schoolers, it's helping them feel accepted and requiring them to eat vegetables. As teenagers, it's helping them avoid the bad crowd. In college, it's not cosigning for the car loan they want to take out. And as adults, it's warning them of the mistakes they're heading toward and offering wise counsel to turn back.

We hear a lot about God being our Protector:

- Exodus 14:14—*The LORD will fight for you, you need only to be still.*
- Psalm 18:2—*The LORD is my rock, my fortress and my deliverer...*
- Psalm 28:7—*The LORD is my strength and my shield...*
- Psalm 71:1—*In you, LORD, I have taken refuge...*
- Matthew 23:37—*"Jerusalem, Jerusalem... how often I have longed to gather your children together, as a hen gathers her chicks under her wings..."*
- Acts 12:11—*"... Now I know without a doubt that the Lord has sent his angel and rescued me..."*

And while God clearly sets an example for us to follow, He goes far beyond mere protection in caring for us, His children. Mere protection is defensive. It doesn't rise to the level of wanting what's best for someone: it simply seeks to avoid what's worst.

Unfortunately, many parents stop their parenting here. Whether the father or mother is physically gone, mentally or emotionally checked out, or simply have too limited a view of their role, they come up short. They protect and preserve life without truly embracing the responsibility of "parenting." It's thinking, *if my kids reach their eighteenth birthday, I've succeeded as a parent.*

As we see in Scripture, protection is an essential role of being a parent. I'll be the first to admit that there are days when preservation of life feels like a victory. But even on those days, I know the calling of a parent is greater.

PROVIDE

Level two of biblical parenting is providing for their physical, emotional, and spiritual growth. As we saw, Jesus was pretty harsh on folks who don't protect their kids, but the apostle Paul isn't much softer on the topic of providing. In 1 Timothy 5:8, Paul writes, *"Anyone who does not provide for their relatives, and especially for their own household, has denied the faith and is worse than an unbeliever."* This is making sure they are fed, clothed, and cared for. As they get older, it's providing for their needs and reasonable wants. It's helping them with their first car and college tuition.

Again, God is the ultimate Provider:

- Genesis 2:9—*The Lord God made all kinds of trees grow out of the ground—trees that were pleasing to the eye and good for food. In the middle of the garden were the tree of life and the tree of the knowledge of good and evil.*
- Deuteronomy 2:7—*. . . These forty years the Lord your God has been with you, and you have not lacked anything.*
- 1 Chronicles 29:12—*Wealth and honor come from you; you are the ruler of all things.*
- Matthew 6:26—*Look at the birds of the air; they do not sow or reap or store away in barns, and yet your heavenly Father feeds them. Are you not much more valuable than they?*
- Philippians 4:19—*And my God will meet all your needs according to the riches of his glory in Christ Jesus.*

While no longer entirely defensive, providing is still very much in the "reactive" arena of parenting. It's meeting needs in the present, but not looking to the future. Like the "protector" parents, the long-term issue with parents who don't push past providing is that they are stuck as providers forever.

This would be fine if the goal, again, was only the sustaining of life. If existence were the goal, protecting and providing would be sufficient. But, as we know, existence is not the goal. God wants us to have *"life to the full"* (John 10:10). To be blessed and to be a blessing (Genesis 12:2). To go out into the world and subdue it (Genesis 1:28).

Dipping our toes into the financial waters, we see in the parable of the talents or bags of gold in Matthew 25:14-30, that God expects growth of the things He's entrusted to us. Notice that the *"wicked, lazy"* and *"worthless"* servant didn't squander or lose the master's money. He didn't lose it in a Ponzi scheme, at the casino, or by reckless living. He simply brought back what the master entrusted to Him without growth. I don't believe this parable is teaching us about the stock market or financial principles at all. It's a life principle. It's teaching us that God wants and expects His kingdom to be grown. It's an expectation He has of us with everything He's entrusted to us—most of all with our children.

PREPARE
This leads us to our full calling as parents. In addition to protecting and providing, we are called to prepare our children to be Christ-following adults. This means we not only defend them and feed them but also teach them to defend and feed themselves—and then others. Protection and provision focus on the moment, but preparation adds the future to our field of vision. It allows for the intentional and gradual shifting of responsibility from us to them. It allows us to surrender the control we clung to in protecting and providing and transfer it to our kids as they become able.

We see God the Preparer woven into the very fabric of the Bible story. God created a perfect paradise and trees with good fruit, giving instructions to Adam and Eve on how to manage it well. He promised to shield Moses and Aaron from Pharoah's wrath and He fed the Israelites enslaved by the Egyptians, but He prepared Moses and Aaron for the responsibility of giving His message to Pharoah. He parted the Red Sea and made manna in the desert but allowed and required the Israelites to gather it. He made the Law to protect and provide but allowed His people to choose whether to follow or ignore it. He sent His own Son into the world with a mission and allowed Him to endure the pain necessary to complete it—without interfering.

And He's given us the autonomy to raise our children however we see best, even when we violate His instruction.

After Erica and I got married in 2007, we bought a house with a big yard and a riding mower. It's now 2022 and I still have that mower. It's not good. The deck has been welded back together. Multiple plug wires and coil replacements. The rear transaxle had to be replaced this summer. The headlights have never worked. A few of the drive pulleys make this weird squealing sound every once in a while, making the neighbors think I ran over one of the chickens. And now the hood is mostly falling off. I've replaced so many spindles that I actually carry inventory in my shed and can change one in NASCAR pit-crew speed.

I've done most of these repairs myself, or at least attempted to. Every once in a while, one of my kids will "want to help" me fix the mower. The truth is, it would be safer for all of us if they didn't. It would be more effective and efficient if they didn't. But then they won't be prepared to work on their own mowers someday, so I let them "help." Allowing them to participate gives them the opportunity to take their natural curiosity and apply it to this important life skill. Sure, it takes at least twice as long because I have to explain everything I'm doing and everything I'm asking them to do. But it's worth it! It's my job as a parent.

Likewise, it would have been safer, more efficient, and more effective if God just spread the gospel Himself, but He sees value in our involvement. I'm not exactly sure what He's preparing us for, but the act of humbling ourselves and obeying Him is somehow preparing us for our eternal future. Somehow, despite our utter ineptitude, a perfect God and His Kingdom are made better by our involvement. I don't get it, but I trust that He does. And if He, our Father, relinquishes a little control so that we can be built up in His image, we should feel compelled to do the same with our children.

As we say at Compass-finances God's way, God has a part, and we have a part. God protects, provides, and prepares; then He gives us the opportunity to participate in His work. We *can't* do His part and He *won't* do ours. As parents, we should embrace this model.

CONTROL AND INFLUENCE

Let's go a little deeper on the topic of control versus influence. Applying the Control/Influence model to our Protect/Provide/Prepare expectations, protection is largely about control, provision a little less so, and preparation relies mainly on influence and the transfer of control. Just as we are called to protect, provide for, and prepare our children, we should be prepared to exercise both control and influence at times.

As we discussed in Chapter 1, our control over our kids begins to dissolve about the time they start walking. It's weak paste by the time they start talking. It evaporates when they start driving. And we can hardly smell the residue when they move out. In many ways, even the control we thought we had was a mirage.

As humans (Christians or otherwise) living in a world with eight billion other people, unpredictable weather patterns, and a million other moving pieces we can't predict, we need to accept that we have almost no control. I can avoid smoking a single cigarette and still get lung cancer. I can drive perfectly and die in a horrific accident. I can do everything right and lose it all (Job 1:1-42:17).

At the end of the day, the only thing I can control is my own choices. I can't control the choices of others and I can't control the outcomes of anything. I can control only what I contribute, and I have to trust God for the rest. I encourage you to take a moment to process that last sentence: it's a game changer.

Although this lack of control is more than a little concerning as it relates to my kids, it's incredibly reassuring to see the influence I can have over them and others. A great example is my dad and me. I'm currently 42 years old. I moved out of my parents' house when I was 18 and never moved back. My dad worked an off shift (4 a.m. to 3 p.m.), so we didn't spend much time together when I was growing up. Even today we have very little in common. I work in full-time ministry and he's not a believer. He golfs and plays tennis; I read and spend time with my wife and kids. He enjoys day trading, and I rarely touch my investments. But a few years ago, I started calling him once a week to try to rebuild the relationship and I find he still influences me.

I think about things he says and how they apply to my life. His perspective changes my perspective even when no one is trying to influence anyone. Hopefully, I have some influence on him as well. But my point is, if he influences me during our one-hour-a-week call after 25 years of living apart, how much more influence do I have with my kids who live in my home? It seems like we're often so focused on control that we miss the opportunity we have with our influence.

Kent Hughes, again, has a great illustration of this point. He says, "Rearing children is like holding a wet bar of soap—too firm a grasp and it shoots from your hand, too loose a grip and it slides away. A gentle but firm hold keeps you in control."

Ironically, our greatest control comes through our influence. By setting a good example, intentionally explaining what and why, and giving them opportunities to participate, I make the most of my influence and fulfill God's expectations as a parent.

But influence is a double-edged sword. While intentionally using it to prepare our children to follow Christ is a great thing, our influence doesn't fade when we're asleep at the wheel either. Like it or not, intentionally or unintentionally, we're constantly influencing our kids.

Do you know why my kids are sarcastic? Because I'm sarcastic. Do you know why I'm sarcastic? Because my dad is sarcastic. For years I didn't even know I was being sarcastic around my kids until one of them was sarcastic back to me. It hit me hard, but it was too late to undo.

I believe this unintentional cause and effect is behind many issues, including the fatherless child cycle that is so prevalent and destructive in our society. A dad skips out on his kid, so the kid learns that's what you do when it gets tough. When they inevitably lose control of a stubborn kid, it's easy to decide they don't want this and skip out too.

The cycle feeds the cycle and it goes on without anyone ever saying, "You know what, I want to be a deadbeat dad someday, just like my dad." The "dad" wasn't even around the kid—but he still influenced him! Even his absence was an influence! This is the most dangerous thing about influence: although you have to embrace and engage to be a positive influence, you don't have to make *any effort at all* to be a negative one.

To be clear, it's not that we should never attempt to control our children. If your child walks up to the edge of the Grand Canyon, you should controllingly grab them and controllingly make it clear never to do that again. Our calling to prepare is not an excuse to not protect or provide. We are called to an additional, higher level of parenting, not to abandon the lower levels altogether.

The final great thing I'll point out about embracing influence in our parenting is the fact that it never goes away. Even as our children grow up, move out, and start their own lives, our ability to influence them never ends. As we move into new stages of life, we have new opportunities to influence our children. As we start to break new ground in our lives, we can better prepare them for when they are our age and go through the same things. As we make a habit of using this influence, we establish those positive baselines we've set our eyes on.

When Erica and I finally did our estate planning last year, we were very transparent about it with our children. We explained what we were doing and why. None of our kids was in a position to do the same, but they now know that's a thing old people do. They heard that our plan was designed to be consistent with Scripture. They heard about how we decided who would care for them if we died sooner than expected. They heard about how we decided who got how much money. Even though they can't follow our example right now—and may not remember any of the specifics when it's their turn—we've influenced them.

They know we're going to die someday. They know we are called to create a plan. They know we believe the Bible has answers to modern-day issues. Have no doubt that these little interactions, stacked up over years, add up. As we pray at dinner every night, talk informally about what we read in the Bible that day, hug and kiss each other and them, we are teaching them what adulthood as a Christian should look like. And in the same way, as my mom talks to me about long-term care costs and planning, she's influencing me to know it's something I should start thinking about now. She shares a perspective I can't relate to or even imagine, teaching me through her wisdom and experiences without ever giving me an instruction. The conversation alone influences me toward being better prepared for the future. It's casual. It's gradual. It's effective.

ACTIVE AND REACTIVE PARENTING

Finally, we'll round out these foundational chapters by revisiting the active and reactive parenting discussion. As we discussed earlier, reactive parenting is defined by addressing situations as they come to us, generally with attempts to control. Active parenting looks ahead at the situations that are likely to come and intentionally prepares children to handle them, generally using influence.

An analogy I like for this comes from my days in Customer Support for an office furniture manufacturer. In their book *The Effortless Experience,* authors Dixon, Toman, and Delisi[3] present and defend that the greatest driver of customer satisfaction and likelihood to buy again isn't price or quality: it's how easy or "effortless" the experience was for the customer. In order to make resolving issues easier, we used their approach called "Next Issue Avoidance." Here's how it's applied:

Not using next issue avoidance

- Customer: "I have an issue with my chair."
- Support Representative: "Can you give me the serial number?"
- Customer: "Where do I find that?"
- Support Representative: "It's on a label under the chair."
- Customer: "There are like 10 labels under the chair . . ."
- Support Representative: "It'll be a label with a barcode and a six-character string on it."
- Customer: "The serial number is CfGw10."
- Support Representative: "Oh, that's not actually the right label. Is there another one with only capital letters and numbers?"
- Customer: "GOD123."

Using next issue avoidance

- Customer: "I have an issue with my chair."
- Support Representative: "Can you give me the serial number? It'll be on a label under the chair with a barcode and a six-character string. There may be more than one label like that, but the one we need will have all capital letters and numbers."
- Customer: "GOD123."

See the difference?! Using Next Issue Avoidance, the Support Rep simply anticipates the next natural issue and proactively gives information to resolve it. This moves the conversation forward in a way that makes the experience feel more effortless to the customer. The chair was still broken at the start and the serial number was still found at the end, but what happened in between was very different and makes the entire interaction less stressful and more productive.

We can think about parenting the same way. As reactive parents, we allow the problem to come to us and do our best to manage the consequences in the moment. As active parents, however, we anticipate where the situation is headed and begin combatting the issue before it even appears.

Most of the issues our children face or will face aren't all that different from what we've gone through. Sure, the expression and details of their issues have changed, but we all have the same fundamental needs and desires.

That's one of the most amazing things about the Bible. The *newest* parts were written nearly 2,000 years ago and its teaching is just as true today as it was then. Most of the Bible was written to the Jews in the Promised Land, but its instructions are just as beneficial to Christians in America, Hungary, or Ghana. Sure, the Bible's Author had better foresight into what was going to happen and what we would need to know, but our past experiences have given us more insight into our children's lives and problems than we often think.

There are two major advantages to active parenting. The first is that we tend to respond better (more like Jesus) to the problems that come up. There are two reasons for this. The first is that we have established a line of communication while the relationship was good and can now approach the situation more comfortably when things are more tense. Talking about complex issues before they are in our face allows us to build rapport and relationship. It allows us to approach a topic lightly as a hypothetical or a true "asking for a friend." Once this line of communication is established, it's much easier and more comfortable to come back around when there are new and more real applications and implications.

The second reason active parents respond better is that the process of thinking ahead allows us to actually think about our response before giving it. By giving ourselves time to think, *how should I explain to my kids why they need to eat broccoli?* we can actually examine our motivations. Is it really because we want them to be healthy or is it more about control and authority? We can formulate a defense of our position that's aligned to our reasons and values. We can consider reasonable arguments they may propose, as well as the unreasonable ones.

Like Next Issue Avoidance in customer service, most parents know what their kids will object to and why. We just need to take some time to think about how we can better communicate our reasons with them. Will your well-intended and well-presented reasoning magically convert your kids into agreeable eaters of broccoli? Will it prevent a meltdown when asked to eat one single butter-doused floret? Probably not, but your approach to the problem will set an example they will naturally follow throughout their lives. They will learn to think through problems, explain their positions, and handle conflict with grace and compassion.

Recall that the first major advantage to active parenting is that we tend to respond better to the problems that come up. The second advantage is even more beneficial: it actually helps prevent the issues we anticipate as parents.

Let's take the dreaded teen pregnancy example from Chapter 1. If the first "birds and bees talk" we have is when our teenage sons or daughters tell us there's a baby coming, we're in deep weeds. Even a miraculous, Spirit-filled, and well-articulated explanation of God's position on conceiving children only inside of marriage will not prevent the baby from being conceived outside of marriage. That ship has sailed. There's nothing we can do to reverse that past decision; now we can only, at best, begin influencing the next decisions.

By actively parenting and preparing our children for life as followers of Jesus before issues come up, we can actually help steer them away from the mistakes they are likely to make. Again, does this mean that explaining God's perspective on sex out of wedlock will stop all teenagers from having sex? Nope. But it will certainly decrease the likelihood, improve your relationship, and influence the way those teenagers approach their own parenting.

As parents, God has entrusted something to us far more valuable than the bag of coins from the parable of the talents. He's given us responsibility for protecting, providing for, and preparing the next generation of Jesus-followers. As active parents who embrace our influence, we can help our children avoid some of the most prevalent threats to their joy and spiritual well-being: the anxiety, materialism, and greed that seem to come naturally to us all. And in doing so, we can use what He's entrusted to us to grow His kingdom for His glory and our good.

THREE BIGGEST TAKEAWAYS FROM THIS CHAPTER

1)

2)

3)

PART 2

A Simple Approach to Parenting

CHAPTER 4

MVP Parenting

> *Fix these words of mine in your hearts and minds; tie them as symbols on your hands and bind them on your foreheads. Teach them to your children, talking about them when you sit at home and when you walk along the road, when you lie down and when you get up.*
>
> DEUTERONOMY 11:18-19

The first time I read *Your Money Counts* by Howard Dayton,[4] I wasn't new to the study of Christian finances. I'd read some of Dave Ramsey's work but wanted more of a biblical perspective. So I studied the Bible itself and nearly drowned trying to swim in the deep end.

I got curious about the topic again and read some other Christian financial perspectives. I have a couple of degrees in education-related fields, so teaching and training methodologies weren't new ground either. And in some of the other theological books I'd read, similar discipleship structures were presented. Despite all that, though, Howard's chapter on parenting struck a chord with me. As I read about what he called "MVP Parenting," it brought it all together for me in a way I understood and felt like I could apply. It was as if he had written the words to explain what I had already known but had never thought deeply enough to realize or articulate.

This sweet spot of being both understandable and applicable is absolutely essential to making something useful and effective. To be successful at anything in life, you need knowledge and discipline. You need to know *what* to do and actually *do it*. If you know what to do but don't actually do it, it's just head knowledge with no results. If you have no clue what you're doing but try it anyway, you generally get chaos. You need to know what to do and do it.

If you want to be a good accountant, learn good accounting practices and follow those principles. Just learning the principles won't do it, and neither will just "giving it your best." If you want to be a great artist, learn the techniques of the craft and practice them. Some may have the ability to do it without training, but most don't. And if you learn to paint but never pick up a brush, what good has it done? If you want to be a great Christian, study the life and teachings of Jesus, and then put them into action. Trying to guess what God wants is perilous (Judges 11) and knowing God's word but not applying it is the worst idea yet (Luke 6:46-48, James 3:1, James 4:17, etc.).

When I need to fix something on the car or lawnmower, I usually start with YouTube—and with extremely mixed results. Sometimes, I find the three-minute video about how to swap an engine on my truck that goes something like this: "So you start by popping the hood. Then, unbolt the engine (guy pointing at the engine like I didn't know where it was), lift it out, and put in the new one. Reattach the bolts and close the hood! That's how you swap out the engine on a 2008 Toyota Tacoma. If you liked this video, hit the thumbs up and subscribe to my channel."

By the end, I really *want* to swap the engine because it looks really easy, but I still don't know how. The opposite is the three-and-a-half-day video that actually shows me every bolt and cable in real time. By the end, I now know exactly how I *could* swap out the engine, but am no longer interested in doing it because it's way more work than I had hoped. Neither extreme drives any sort of positive result.

This is what I love about MVP Parenting. It's simple enough to both understand and apply, it's just as applicable to big stuff as it is little, and it encourages us to embrace influence over control as we parent actively rather than reactively. MVP Parenting consists of providing Modeling, Verbal Instruction, and Practical Opportunities in anything we want to see in and for our children. In education, it aligns to the idea that you show, tell, and try. In broad-based discipleship, Robert Coleman in *Master Plan of Evangelism*[5] describes it as demonstrating, instructing, and delegating—all in the package of an easy-to-remember acronym!

As we dig a little deeper into MVP Parenting, we need to recognize that influencing our children toward living out biblical principles is a lot like reading and applying the Proverbs. As BibleProject[6] puts it, they're probabilities, not promises. They aren't guarantees of success but rather best practices of living within God's creation.

The Bible certainly offers us many promises, but that's not the purpose of the Proverbs. Let's take our anchor verse from Chapter One (Proverbs 22:6) as an example. If we train up our children in the way they should go, is God promising they will never stray? No. If we don't train them up in the way they should go, are they doomed to failure and without hope? Also no. But we shouldn't dismiss the wisdom shared with us in the Proverbs simply because the result isn't guaranteed.

Yes, it's possible that I could get lung cancer if I'm a non-smoker. And yes, I could smoke for 50 years and not get cancer. But it's prudent and wise to not smoke if I'd prefer to not get lung cancer. It's not a matter of promise but of probability. And if I want to give my children the best chance of avoiding the dangerous and painful pitfalls of greed and materialism, I should train them up in the way they should go, viewing money and possessions as a way to honor and glorify God.

There are some basic ingredients to financial management that I'll introduce now. I want to be clear, though, that our goal in life, and therefore in this book, is not simply sound financial management. That would make our life about money, which it's not. That's the wide and well-worn path of the world, but it's not the path we're called to travel as followers of Jesus.

Our goal is to bring glory to God through a healthier relationship with Him, made possible by a healthier relationship with money. If, however, our only result from this book is a wealthy, debt-free family with a weak relationship with God, we have not achieved our goal.

In general, following God's instructions for handling money and possessions will turn out better for us financially, but that's missing the point. The tactical management of money is important, but it's only a single ingredient in the final product, not the final product itself. You wouldn't be happy if you ordered a pizza and were brought a bowl of flour. Yes, the flour is important to a pizza. In fact, it's essential. But it's not pizza. Please don't allow money to become the central point of your financial discipleship journey. Your goal must remain Christ-centered, with finances kept in their proper place as one of many ingredients added at the proper time and in proper proportion to achieve the goal of bringing glory to God.

So, let's dive into an overview of five basic ingredients: Income, Expenses, Plans, Execution, and Accounting. Each presents unique challenges and opportunities. In later chapters we'll flesh out the MVP approach for each one with Modeling, Verbal Instruction, and Practical Opportunities.

INCOME

Income is exactly what you think. It's the money you receive. Could be from work, investments, gifts, or social programs. We're going to consider all money that comes in to be "Income." We could certainly fine-tune this definition, but we need to keep it simple for a few reasons. First, it's easier for us to apply if it's simple. A very easy way to ensure failure at something new is to make it complicated. Maybe later we can handle a definition where gifts fall into some other category, but the simplest definition will be the best definition for now.

Second, it's easier for us to teach our children things that are simple. The last class I took to complete my Mathematics degree required us to *prove* that one plus one equals two. It took about six weeks and several hundred pages of a notebook. But that's not how we teach our kids that one plus one equals two. We keep it simple and give them enough explanation to make it true and helpful, not to make them confused experts.

Third, micromanaging the definition doesn't have much relevance in a child's life. They likely have an allowance and occasional gifts, but no investments or social-program inflows, so why confuse the matter? Our starting place and minimal requirement as parents is a system our kids can understand and replicate. As adults, our full system may be more complex, but we should still be able to show and tell our children examples from our lives that make sense and apply to their simpler context.

Aside from setting the general limits of our giving, saving, and spending, income is also important because it is often a source of frustration for us, an attitude we can easily transfer to our children if we aren't intentional. The truth is that work is a gift from God. Cliché perhaps, but that doesn't make it any less true. We often connect work to the Fall in Genesis 3, but that's an unfortunate error. Work existed before the Fall. In fact, work existed since the beginning.

One of the first attributes we learn about God is that He is productive, that is, He works. Before anything else, God existed perfectly in community with Himself. But He wanted to make something. Actually, He wanted to make EVERYTHING! After creating for six days, Genesis 2:3 tells us God *"rested from all His work."*

When God suggested on Day 6 that He make man *"in our [His] image,"* one of the attributes we inherited was God's productivity. After creating us in His image, Genesis 1:28 says He blessed us and told us, *"Be fruitful and increase in number; fill the earth and subdue it."* That is, He gave us a job.

Because of the Fall, work became difficult and frustrating, but that's not how it was meant to be. That was one of the consequences of sin.

It's essential for our children that we teach them the true value of income and work, aside from the lifestyle it allows. Follow me on this. If our kids work 40 hours per week, 49 weeks per year for 50 years, they will have worked 98,000 hours in their lifetime. Imagine if our kids could be taught to properly dedicate those hours to God and spend those 98,000 hours in worship rather than frustration! That's a baseline worth building, but it has to start with us.

EXPENSES

For the sake of this conversation, expenses are the ways money goes out. We'll discuss in much greater detail some of the various types of expenses, but for now we'll include giving and spending. Saving will be a major topic for later, but saving is just delayed giving or spending (what you save now will be given or spent later), so we won't muddy the water with it yet. Expenses are an essential point of discussion because they are the outward expression of our inward priorities.

My oldest son is an interesting financial character. He's an earner and saver who also puts great value in expensive things. The way it plays out is that if *you* are paying, he wants the best. If *he* is paying, the bottom of the barrel will generally do just fine.

One day we were driving through the Chicago suburbs and he was pointing out all the really nice things (cars, houses, pools, etc.). At one point he exclaimed, "How do all these people have so much money?" In that moment, I said something without ever having thought about it before, but have repeated it a hundred times since. "Yeah, but it's important to understand that the stuff people have doesn't represent the money they *have*. It actually represents the money they *no longer* have."

I think we can all relate to this. We probably all have family members (we may even *be* those family members) who have the *appearance* of financial wealth but very little *actual* financial wealth. Their financial wealth has been exchanged for nice stuff and lots of it. On the other hand, we also have family members (hopefully we *are* those family members) who live in simple houses, drive simple cars, and carry out very unimpressive lives—but have surprising financial wealth.

As Christians, we are called to lives of simplicity and contentment, not placing our value in stuff. There's nothing wrong with having nice things if God has provided for them, but they should testify *to*, rather than distract *from*, His provision of spiritual life.

Jesus switched the whole paradigm with one simple command in Matthew 6:20, *"Store up for yourselves treasures in heaven."* We also see the negative example of this principle in the story of the rich young man in Matthew 19. He comes to Jesus for instruction on how to obtain eternal life. Unfortunately, he discovers that his emotional and spiritual connection to his stuff prevents it.

Our expenses are outward expressions of our inner priorities and desires. If we are to bring glory to God through our handling of money and possessions, our priorities and desires need to be aligned and realigned to the priorities and desires of God as expressed in Scripture.

PLANS

Plans are essential to managing our finances God's way because they require us to think intentionally about our income and expenses, making decisions about how to best honor God. Plans, as they relate to our finances, come in many sizes and by many names. Our weekly or monthly plan is called our budget. Our plan for leaving money behind after we die is an estate plan. Determining the financial details of our retirement is our retirement plan. While each is different in scope, they all require and accomplish the same basic things. They require us to measure, approximate, or predict our income and make intentional choices on how we will put that money to use.

Like the Active/Reactive Parenting conversation, we generally make better financial decisions when we've thought through our options before actually being confronted with a choice. Every spending decision forces us to choose. Since money is a limited commodity (we only have a certain amount at any time), our choice to spend on one thing limits our ability to spend on another. If I choose to eat out at lunch today, I am choosing to not do something another day. Maybe that means I can't go out to eat tomorrow or maybe that means I kick the can down the road and leave $12 less to my kids. But at some point, the choice to spend today means a choice to not spend another day.

Debt can muddy the water, but it doesn't change this basic fact. If I borrow money to buy a house today, I choose not to do other things for the next 30 years. We may be used to this trade-off because debt is so common to us, but for those of us who have gotten out of debt, it's amazing to see the amount of income you have access to without a mortgage, car payments, and student loans. Whether we pay today or over time, good interest rate or bad, our choice to spend money in one place is also a choice to *not* spend in another.

Most of us, without a plan, will quickly fall off track. Working on a plan early (before being forced into limited options because of spending with no plan) gives us time to earnestly pray for God's wisdom (James 3:17). We have time to seek and consider wise counsel (Proverbs 15:22), and to test our own convictions—both how good our reasons are and how badly we want something—(James 4:3). While plans are certainly encouraged (Proverbs 20:18, Proverbs 21:5, Luke 14:28-29), they should also be guided by God, presented to God, and subject to God's approval or redirection (Luke 12:20-21).

EXECUTION

Just as knowledge without discipline is pointless, so is a good plan without good execution. If we make plans for where and on what we will spend our money, we also need plans for how we will stay true to our plans. We should build in both accountability and flexibility.

At Compass-finances God's way, we're often asked what the best budgeting tool is. FaithFi, Every Dollar, Mint, Excel, paper and pencil? Our answer is simple: Whichever one you'll actually use.

When Erica and I made our first budget, we decided on the envelope-system and made envelopes for everything. We had an envelope for food, another for toiletries, a third for dog food, another for cleaning supplies, along with a few dozen others. You can see how this played out. We went to Walmart and bought cereal, toothpaste, dog food, and dishwasher detergent and had to be those people who ran four transactions. After two trips like this, we were over it. Yes, we needed tight accountability, but we needed to rearrange some things. We stuck with the envelope system and cash, but decided we'd bucket everything we would "normally" buy at the grocery store into one envelope called "Necessities." This allowed us to better execute our plan because it fit our lives in a way we could actually live out.

ACCOUNTING

This final ingredient is one of the more common but misunderstood elements. Many people (including me for a long time) view budgeting and tracking as the same thing. They are not. You can create a budget but not keep it. And you can track expenses without actually having a plan. Both are necessary but they aren't the same. You need to create a plan ahead of time. And you need to take an accounting of your execution afterward. Both/and, not either/or.

Like planning, there are many ways to track. Like all other ingredients, simpler is better to start. We'll discuss it more later, but this is one of the reasons Erica and I, after 13 years of budgeting and tracking, stick with cash and envelopes for our primary currency. We've tried multiple times to take advantage of credit card deals and miles, but tracking always becomes too difficult. We have to juggle receipts with notes, reconcile spending categories online several days after the purchases are made, and try to keep track of how much is left in a budget line item. At the end of each attempt, we've reverted back to cash and leave the credit card benefits for someone with better skills in planning and execution.

This isn't a biblical choice; you can go another way if you want, but cash is simple, real, and has natural accounting and accountability built in since you can't make tracking mistakes. When the envelope's empty, you're out. You can argue all you want and look waaaay down in there to see if something's stuck in the bottom, but if it's empty, you're out.

Cash is also essential because as you train your child to handle money well, you likely won't be giving them a credit card. In order to model and explain the right behavior for them, you will need to function in some capacity in *their* primary currency—cash.

Enough about currency choices for now. Accounting simply requires you to compare your original plan with your actual execution. This allows you to see where you have succeeded and failed. It informs your choices for the next plan.

It may seem like an overreach to cite Romans 14:12, *"So then, each of us will give an account of ourselves to God,"* and apply it to the area of finances, but I believe it's a perfect fit. If we recognize the goal of our finances, our parenting, and everything else—as bringing glory to God—then not staying disciplined to the necessary steps of achieving that goal is going to come up in our account to God.

Accounting is also powerful for exposing the secret vices not even you knew you had. Early in Erica's and my budgeting, I was traveling by car a lot for work. I blew through my entire envelope of personal spending money the first week of the month just buying gas station fountain drinks. I had never done the math on how much that cost, but I assure you I made different spending choices after that.

Likewise, our financial meltdown was largely driven (as far as I can tell) by a lack of accounting. We had a plan but apparently didn't follow it. To this day, we have no clue where the money went. We had a good plan, but no accounting to make sure we stayed true to the plan.

As we'll learn in the chapters to come, each of these ingredients has implications on how we train our children to be godly stewards of God's money. We'll discover how each can be modeled, verbalized, and practiced in order to achieve our goal of glorifying God and raising children who do the same.

THREE BIGGEST TAKEAWAYS FROM THIS CHAPTER

1)

2)

3)

CHAPTER 5

Modeling

Follow my example, as I follow the example of Christ.

1 CORINTHIANS 11:1

I find this simple starting point of MVP Parenting to be the most difficult and relentless. The truth is, if we want to influence our children toward God's financial best practices, it starts with our example. I know some of you now feel like this book was a bait and switch—"Wait a second! I bought this book so that my *kids* could surrender their finances to God, not so I could!" Sorry, sort of. That's why this book isn't titled, *Financial Discipleship for Your Kids but Not You.* As difficult, annoying, and inconvenient as this step may be, it's essential for your children's development, as well as yours.

As you've probably noticed, your children are always watching and learning. Whatever it is you're doing, they're paying attention and soaking it up. Even before they knew they were doing it, they were mirroring your facial expressions, mannerisms, and voice inflections.

As they grew older, they grew more intentional and selective about what behaviors they adopted. Even while they were choosing to intentionally reject some, they continued to take note of your behaviors and attitudes in every area of your life. Although your intentional and unintentional influence may decrease as your children age, it will never disappear completely. We need to embrace this influence to help our kids grow toward Christ as opposed to any other direction.

One of the most difficult things about providing good Modeling for our children is that it is a nonstop endeavor. We can pause Verbal Instruction by not explaining what we're doing and why. We can choose to not provide Practical Opportunities if we want. But we can never stop Modeling. Even our inaction is modeling—at the very least, the behavior of inaction.

When one of our kids says something snarky to Erica, I have a few choices. I can correct them, I can blow up on them, or I can do nothing. The first option models self-control as well as love and respect for Erica and my kids. The second option models love and respect for Erica, a lack of self-control, and disrespect for my kids. The third option models an abandonment of my role as leader of the family as well as a lack of love and respect for Erica and apathy about my kids' development.

There is not an option that doesn't model *something*.

As Erica and I were talking with some friends a few months back, they expressed frustration that their teenage son no longer wanted to go to church. "We've dropped him off at Youth Group every week for years and even encourage him to go on Sunday mornings, so we don't know why he's so against it now."

From outside of this conversation, the problem is obvious, "You drop him off every week but you don't actually go to anything yourself. Why do you expect him to value it if you don't?"

I think we all are prone to do the same. We want our children to have a better life than we've had, to avoid the pain we experienced. To be more focused on their faith and less focused on popularity. To read the Bible more and social media less. But do we want it badly enough to put our money where our mouth is? Or as the Bible puts it, to put our treasure where our heart is (Matthew 6:21)?

PERSONAL BENEFITS TO MODELING

In addition to the example we set for our children, modeling also offers significant benefits for *us*. The first is to help us be certain we understand what we're about to teach our kids. In Matthew 7:4-5, Jesus sharply corrects the Pharisees for judging others without first addressing the sin in their own lives. He instructs us there to, *"first take the plank out of your own eye, and then you will see clearly to remove the speck from your brother's eye."*

Notice what Jesus was saying to the Pharisees. It wasn't that they shouldn't point out the failures of others, but that they needed to first address their own failures. Once they had addressed the issue in their own lives, they were then better able to help others. When we first model the behaviors we want to see in our children, we can more effectively lead them, because we, ourselves, know the way.

The second benefit to us as we provide modeling is that we take seriously Jesus' instruction to put what we've learned into practice. Skye Jethani, in his challenging but true book *What if Jesus Was Serious*,[7] correctly points out a common misapplication of the parable of the wise and foolish builders found in Matthew 7:24-27.

> *"Therefore everyone who hears these words of mine and puts them into practice is like a wise man who built his house on the rock. The rain came down, the streams rose, and the winds blew and beat against that house; yet it did not fall, because it had its foundation on the rock. But everyone who hears these words of mine and does not put them into practice is like a foolish man who built his house on sand. The rain came down, the streams rose, and the winds blew and beat against that house, and it fell with a great crash."*

Many Christians, he points out, believe this parable means that the wise builder (who built his house on the rock) is the one who believes in Jesus, and the foolish builder (who built his house on the sand) is the nonbeliever. If we read this parable with fresh eyes, however, we clearly see that it isn't *belief* in Jesus that makes a builder wise or foolish, it's the *obedience* to Jesus that does. If we as parents believe it is wise for our children to apply biblical financial principles in *their* lives but don't apply them in *our* lives, which builder do you suppose we are? I think we know the answer.

KEY ELEMENTS OF MODELING

There are two key elements in good modeling. The first is fairly intuitive: actually *doing* the thing you want your children to do. If you want your kids to love reading, you're going to need to read. If you want your kids to sing, you should sing. If you want your kids to pray, you need to pray. If you want your kids to be kind to your spouse (and theirs someday), you need to be kind to your spouse (and theirs someday). And if you want your kids to be faithful financial stewards, it needs to start with you. Sure, your child may respond well to the age-old, "Do as I say, not as I do" or the more accurate, "Do as I mean, not as I say," but it's a long shot. And they might simply discover the best practices on their own, but modeling the behaviors yourself is the most effective way to accomplish this goal.

The second element of effective modeling is doing it in a way your children will see and notice. This one isn't as obvious. If you read, but not when and where they can see you, you haven't actually modeled it. If you beautifully serenade God, but only in the car when you're alone, they can't possibly soak it up. If you show affection to your spouse only in private, you can't expect to positively impact their baseline. And if you want your children to understand the importance of handling money God's way, you need to live it out in front of them.

Creating an intentional plan for how you will exhibit the behaviors and attitudes you want to see in your children is an essential step in training them in godliness. The truth is, the behaviors and attitudes our kids will learn from us unintentionally probably won't be the ones we *want* them to learn.

On one side of this, it seems disingenuous to put on a show in front of our children, pretending to be better people than we are. On the other side, though, being a parent gives us yet another reason to be more like Christ.

I should have stopped swearing when I entered into a relationship with Christ (Ephesians 4:29), but I stopped when I had kids. I should have stopped speeding when I read that Christians should honor authorities and obey the law (Romans 13:1), but I stopped when one of my kids called me on it. In an effort to be the role model my children needed, I did what I should have done anyway. In that way, God has used parenting to disciple *me* so that I could be in a better position to disciple my children.

GOD, OUR EXAMPLE

Seeing God as our example may seem obvious enough to not need mentioning, but the pattern in Scripture, especially with how Jesus modeled, is significant. Jesus was sent, not only to be a perfect sacrifice, but also to be our perfect example. Before Jesus spoke and taught, He *did*. He loved before He told others to love. He prayed before instructing others to pray. He healed before sending others to heal. And He gave His life before expecting us to. Jesus consistently modeled modeling before ever explaining or commanding anything. Paul captures this in our anchor verse, 1 Corinthians 11:1, when he says, *"Follow my example, as I follow the example of Christ."*

This was the power of Jesus' mission. God showed that He wasn't some far-off deity hovering around in the spiritual realm casually watching this show from a distance. You've probably heard about the difference between the chicken and the pig at breakfast. The chicken was involved but the pig was committed. God didn't start this ball rolling and walk away. He didn't just leave us a book of instructions and let us figure it out from there. He sent us an example to follow.

That's why Hebrews 4:15 points out that *"we do not have a high priest who is unable to empathize with our weaknesses, but we have one who has been tempted in every way, just as we are—yet he did not sin."* He was so invested in His ultimate creation that He became human so He could perfectly model faithfulness, righteousness, and godliness.

If He hadn't experienced what we experience, been hurt like we've been hurt, been hungry like we're hungry, and tempted as we're tempted, we might have an excuse—though not a good one. But that's not the God we serve. We serve a God who is so passionate about our redemption and salvation that He came down Himself to *show* us how to live. And much like that pig at breakfast, He was committed, all-in, to death, even death on the cross (Philippians 2:8).

So if Jesus was sent to be our perfect example, God values modeling. And if Jesus' first step was to *show*, rather than *tell*, Jesus demonstrated modeling. And if we are to be more like Christ, we must model like Jesus modeled.

A WORD OF WARNING

As we consider how to demonstrate faithful behaviors in a way our children can see, it's important we first get our hearts right. Jesus, in His Sermon on the Mount, gave us a very direct and stern warning about putting on a show for the sake of being seen as holy.

In Matthew 6:1, Jesus says, *"Be careful not to practice your righteousness in front of others to be seen by them. If you do, you will have no reward from your Father in heaven."* In verse 2, He goes on to say, *"So when you give to the needy, do not announce it with trumpets, as the hypocrites do in the synagogues and on the streets, to be honored by others."* Then in verses 5 and 6, *"And when you pray, do not be like the hypocrites, for they love to pray standing in the synagogues and on the street corners to be seen by others. Truly I tell you, they have received their reward in full. But when you pray, go into your room, close the door and pray to your Father, who is unseen. Then your Father, who sees what is done in secret, will reward you."* Again in verse 16, *"When you fast, do not look somber as the hypocrites do, for they disfigure their faces to show others they are fasting. Truly I tell you, they have received their reward in full."*

While these verses instruct us to hide our acts of obedience and faith, the instruction should be applied as Jesus intended, to our motivations rather than the act and audience itself. I do not believe Jesus would say we should never be kind in front of others or help the needy with others around or pray in public or be around other people during our time of fasting. In fact, Jesus Himself did all these things, and much more, in front of large crowds. What He's speaking to here is our intent. If our intent in praying in front of our children is to merit their praise, we violate Jesus' instruction. But if our intent is to teach and train our children in faithful communion with God, we actually follow His example and instruction.

We'll go much deeper into these in later chapters, but here are some questions to help you start thinking about what you want for your children and how you can model those behaviors.

- What do my children need to know about work and income to be faithful followers of Jesus and how can I demonstrate those in a way they can see?
- What do my children need to know about giving and spending to be faithful followers of Jesus and how can I demonstrate those in a way they can see?
- What do my children need to know about planning and budgeting to be faithful followers of Jesus and how can I demonstrate those in a way they can see?
- What do my children need to know about executing a financial plan to be faithful followers of Jesus and how can I demonstrate those in a way they can see?
- What do my children need to know about accounting for their finances to be faithful followers of Jesus and how can I demonstrate those in a way they can see?

THREE BIGGEST TAKEAWAYS FROM THIS CHAPTER

1)

2)

3)

CHAPTER 6

Verbal Instruction

Teach them to your children, talking about them when you sit at home and when you walk along the road, when you lie down and when you get up.

DEUTERONOMY 11:19

This second component of MVP Parenting, Verbal Instruction, is probably one most of us already embrace, though maybe not as intentionally as we should. Despite the instruction given in James 1:19, we are often quick to speak, especially with our kids. As we try to exert control rather than influence, we jump the gun by putting "telling" before "showing," offering commands rather than insight, and orders rather than guidance.

PERSONAL BENEFITS OF VERBAL INSTRUCTION
The greatest personal benefit to providing verbal instruction is that we further enhance and enrich our own knowledge and motivations behind what we do and want our children to do. If we are going to explain something to our kids, we should think through the key elements we'll discuss next as we solidify our resolve to teach our kids.

A simple "Because I said so" isn't going to cut it. We don't have to be experts, but we'll have to know what we know—and what we *don't* know—and be ready to articulate both. It's commonly said that one of the best ways to learn something is to try to teach it to others. We'll find that to be true in the area of money and possessions. We have to organize our thoughts, anticipate their questions and objections, and be ready for the unavoidable curveball our kids will throw at us. All of this preparation helps us better understand the changes we want to see in our children's lives.

Another benefit to providing verbal instruction is that we make ourselves more accountable in our own practice of the right behaviors. That may not sound like a big selling point, but none of us wants to be a hypocrite, especially when it comes to our children. We may lack wisdom in some areas, and discipline in others, but we all want to be seen by our children as having integrity.

By giving detailed explanations of our behaviors and motivations to our children, we put them on alert to watch us even more closely. This amplifies our reasons for not compromising our determination to pursue holiness. As we will discuss later, accountability partners are essential to successfully staying true to our plans and commitments. Providing verbal instruction puts our kids in this position and puts their tendency to never stop watching us to good use!

KEY ELEMENTS OF VERBAL INSTRUCTION

Used properly, Verbal Instruction brings "color" to our Modeling, as our intentional explanations open the door for our ever-curious kids to ask questions. And as with Modeling, this step is made up of two key elements: *what* and *why*.

More than anything else, explaining *what* we are doing invites a child into our activities and into a conversation. One particular study (https://amorebeautifulquestion.com/why-do-kids-ask-so-many-questions-but-more-importantly-why-do-they-stop/) shows that preschool children ask just under 100 questions per day, dropping to around 25 by the time they graduate high school. This is a good thing when it's because they are developing critical thinking skills and a library of their own experiences to look back on. But it can also create an impediment to them as they encounter things they have no frame of reference for but have grown uncomfortable asking us questions. By offering an explanation of what we are doing, whether simple or elaborate, we open that conversation back up, giving them permission to ask questions on that topic—or the next one they're curious about.

Author and speaker Cory Carlson's[8] family has taken this concept to the extreme. Faced with the reality that the world is happy to answer any question their kids have, he and his wife have decided they will answer any question their kids ask. *ANY question*! In his book *Win at Home First*, he recounts explaining homosexuality to their teenage daughter because her aunt married a woman and the daughter asked how that worked. Awkward, yes. But Cory's got the right idea here. If they ask us about a topic and we dismiss them because we're uncomfortable answering it, they walk away still curious. Do we really think they're going to drop it because we effectively evaded their questions? No. They're going to google it or ask their friends (who googled it). The blind will lead the blind and they will, together, fall into a pit (Matthew 15:14).

Let's take the conversation away from the extreme topics our children will someday explore and back to the "normal" line of questioning they have. When we sit down to review our monthly budget, we can simply offer them the explanation that, "Every month, Mom and I sit down and plan how we're going to use the money God has given us."

When the offering plate passes by and we notice our children looking curiously, it's a great time to explain what's happening. When we're out in the garage fixing the lawnmower again and we see our kid standing at a distance staring at us like we have a third arm, we can offer the explanation that the idler pulley was making a funny noise so we're going to fix it. These types of explanations invite them into the life of a responsible adult and give them permission to ask questions.

The second element of good verbal instruction is explaining *why* we are doing what we're doing. Kids have incredible imaginations. It's amazing how confined the minds of adults become as we grow older. We take all our experiences and understanding and create proverbial boxes in our minds, only to later challenge one another to "think outside the box" for new ideas. These boxes have incredible advantages for helping us organize and classify things for future reference and use, but they also limit our creativity. Kids have few mental boxes, resulting in both an advantage and disadvantage.

When I went on a mission trip to Haiti, it was amazing to see the imaginations of kids there. Although our kids here in the US have incredible imaginations relative to US adults, Haitian kids take it to a whole new level.

We would drive around from village to village making balloon animals, much to their amazement and amusement. The best part, however, was that when their balloon animal popped, they quickly discovered they had a new toy! Their dog, rabbit, elephant, or giraffe no longer existed, but now they had a streamer, bow and arrow, or just a thing that stretched a lot. They would hear the pop, pause for a second, and create a new use in just a few seconds. They never thought to ask for another balloon animal. In their minds, they still had a fun toy, just not the one they started with.

This is how children see the world. Their lack of experience makes every object or event into an endless world of possibilities. And while this is great for problem-solving and the creation of new "outside the box" ideas, it can be detrimental if our goal is to pass along a specific piece of wisdom.

Let's take giving at church as an example. If you attend an old-school church, the offering plate comes by and you drop some cash or a check in. How many different explanations can your child think of about what's happening here? Maybe you're loaning the church money. Maybe God requires you to pay rent for your chair. Maybe we're supposed to pay for the coffee and candy we consume on Sunday mornings. Maybe going to heaven costs money, like going to the movies, but when you die, you can't take money, so you pay it now while you're still alive because if you don't pay it now they'll throw you out and take one of your shoes so you have to walk back to earth with only one shoe (and nothing could be worse than having to walk back from heaven with only one shoe, except maybe walking back from heaven with one shoe and the other shoe untied . . .).

If your church is more modern and you pick up your phone to text your tithe, do they know who you're texting? If you have a recurring gift set up, what sort of reasons can they come up with about why other people give and you don't?

The imaginations of our kids are amazing, but left to wander on their own, they can come up with some very incorrect conclusions. Explaining why we do what we do allows them to not only observe what we're doing but to learn the correct reason why.

With Modeling, we intentionally choose behaviors that set the right Jesus-like example for our children. With Verbal Instruction, we take the guesswork out of the demonstration and connect it back to our faith, love, and obedience to Jesus. "This is the offering time. Everything we have has been given to us by God. And even though He doesn't need the money, He lets us help. That's why we pass the plate around. We give online though, so we just tell the bank to send money instead of putting the money in the plate."

GOD, OUR INSTRUCTOR

As with Modeling, God is our perfect teacher of how and why to provide Verbal Instruction. On the whole, if Modeling alone were sufficient, God could have traveled with the Israelites in the desert, sent Jesus as our example, and left it at that. But He didn't. He also left us detailed explanations and instructions.

Let's start in the Old Testament. God, Himself, was holy (He modeled holiness) but then gave *us* instructions on how to be holy. In Leviticus 11:44, God says, *"I am the Lord your God; consecrate yourselves and be holy, because I am holy."* He then goes on to explain how the Israelites could actually go about becoming holy in service to Him. What to eat, how to treat skin diseases, what to do about mildew, good employment practices, how to treat foreigners, and on and on. It wasn't enough for God to just demonstrate holiness. It was more effective for God to both show and tell.

As you quickly flip through the Gospels in your modern-day

New Testament, you will immediately notice there's a lot of red (Jesus' words). After modeling a behavior, Jesus consistently explained what and why, often to the amazement of His followers and disapproval of His adversaries. After praying, He explained praying (Luke 11). After healing, He explained healing (Mark 9). After dying on the cross, He explained true sacrifice of self (John 21).

Jesus came to live a perfect life as our example, but God still saw it worthwhile to have the Epistles written, adding a more detailed explanation of how to live like Jesus in a physical world *after* Jesus. If an example had been enough, we would have only the Gospels without the red parts—no explanations. Fortunately, we've been given so much more so that we can more closely replicate not only the behaviors but the heart of God.

A WORD OF WARNING

Like with Modeling, there is the risk of misusing our Verbal Instruction and actually contradicting the example and instruction of Scripture. I see two major mistakes we can make, though I'm sure there are many others.

The first is conveying inaccurate or inconsistent information. In the corporate world, the rule was, if you were asked a question and didn't know the answer, you should tell them you don't know the answer, but that you would find the answer. After the meeting, find the answer and report back.

This rule is good with children too. Remember that they're always learning from you. If the example you set is to offer an answer even if it's wrong, they will learn to do the same. Best case, they walk away with incorrect knowledge of the truth (not a great outcome). Worst case, they end up spotting your mistake and walk away not trusting you, believing that's how adults respond (a terrible outcome).

In Matthew 22:29-30, Jesus calls out the Sadducees for this very thing. They wanted to test Jesus by asking him a ridiculous theoretical question presented as a meaningful theological question—just like our kids do.

The details of Jesus' response are irrelevant to this topic, but He opens with something *very* relevant. Jesus says, "*You are in error because you do not know the Scriptures or the power of God.*" This may not sound too harsh, but this is a pretty big insult. The guys He's talking to are leaders of the church, well-respected teachers who took the firm and uncompromising position that there were no spiritual beings and there would be no resurrection of the dead. These were men of authority whose teachings were taken as the truth, but they hadn't thought through their positions sufficiently.

Like the students of these teachers in the Bible, our children consider us to be knowledgeable and trustworthy. If we don't know the answer, we should openly tell them so, even if we follow it with "but I think . . ." This models and communicates honesty and humility, something Jesus would be proud of.

A second mistake is using our explanations to manipulate others for our own benefit. The most common ways this shows up is knowingly answering incorrectly or leaving out some parts of our answer for our personal gain rather than to simplify something complex for their benefit.

Jesus corrected this in the Pharisees as He interacted with them. They, like the Sadducees, were well-respected teachers. They commonly modified or expanded biblical laws and harshly judged anyone who didn't follow their version of the law. At times, I get to thinking they likely meant well. Probably just trying to simplify and clarify. But then I'm confronted with Jesus' own words. Take a moment and read Matthew 23. Jesus is clear that the Pharisees didn't just make a minor oversight. Their hearts were hardened, and they had intentionally manipulated the law and their teaching of the law for their own advantage.

As we explain our actions and intentions, it's important that we remain focused on bringing glory to God through the training of our children. We must be humble, honest, and open—as Jesus was.

Again, here are some questions to help you start thinking about what you want for your children and how you can explain those behaviors. The Goals are still the same, but we've moved from Modeling to Verbalizing.

- What do my children need to know about work and income to be faithful followers of Jesus and how can I explain those in an engaging way they can understand?
- What do my children need to know about giving and spending to be faithful followers of Jesus and how can I explain those in an engaging way they can understand?
- What do my children need to know about planning and budgeting to be faithful followers of Jesus and how can I explain those in an engaging way they can understand?
- What do my children need to know about executing a financial plan to be faithful followers of Jesus and how can I explain those in an engaging way they can understand?
- What do my children need to know about accounting for their finances to be faithful followers of Jesus and how can I explain those in an engaging way they can understand?

THREE BIGGEST TAKEAWAYS FROM THIS CHAPTER

1)

2)

3)

CHAPTER 7

Practical Opportunities

*Therefore go and make disciples of all nations,
baptizing them in the name of the Father and of
the Son and of the Holy Spirit.*

MATTHEW 28:19

The final step in MVP Parenting is providing Practical Opportunities for our children to practice what we've shown and told them. This step is the proverbial icing on the cake, and no cake is complete without icing! We have now engaged their curiosity by Modeling godly behaviors. We've motivated them with good Jesus-focused Verbal Instruction. It's time to solidify the lesson by offering them the opportunity to practice what we've preached.

KEY BENEFITS TO PROVIDING PRACTICAL OPPORTUNITIES

I'll offer three key benefits to this, but please know the benefits are endless. The first benefit is what I alluded to in the previous paragraph. As we roll directly from Modeling into Verbal Instruction, our kids' curiosity and interest are peaked, making them much more likely to want to take a shot themselves.

After seeing us under the mower and then hearing us tell them about the idler pulley and the crazy noise it makes, they naturally want to see, hear, and feel it themselves. If you just walked into the living room and said, "Who wants to fix the mower?" you would get mixed results. Some kids will want to because they're bored, but others would prefer to stay bored. If they've stopped to watch you and stayed long enough to hear about what you're doing and why, they're hooked.

The second benefit is one of supervision. By intentionally providing opportunities rather than waiting for whatever just happens, you can orchestrate some of the events, ensuring the assignment they take on is appropriate for their age and skill. You're able to stay close to them, making sure they do good work; stopping, correcting, and encouraging them when they make mistakes; congratulating and thanking them for their job well done when they complete a task.

Nothing is more likely to get a kid (or adult) to quit something than experiencing complete and total failure on their first try. Maybe they don't have the dexterity to get the bolt into the first few threads, but once you get it started, they can turn the ratchet a few times. Maybe they can't mix the batter when the flour and liquid are still separated, but after you've got them mixed a little, they can stir a few times. These little successes stacked up over time will build not only their knowledge and skill set but also their confidence.

Finally, the greatest benefit is time together. As adults, we have a lot on our plates. As Christian parents, we have even more. But as we go about our normal adult life, inviting our children to help allows us to get done what needs to get done—and spend time together—all at once.

A good example of this is the mowing ministry I have with our oldest son. One day he saw me mowing and wanted to learn how. I explained it all to him and gave him a chance. I walked right in front of him to make sure he was operating the mower safely, was keeping his lines somewhat straight, and to tell him when he left a "mohawk" (our term for the strip of grass you miss between passes). After a summer or two, he graduated to the riding mower, with a similar regimen of training.

Around that same time, an older lady at church asked if I'd mow her lawn, so he and I went out and mowed for a her a few times. Her neighbor asked how much we charged. I told him we were just a couple of Christians showing Jesus' love, so if he needed his yard mowed, we'd be happy to help. A few weeks later, the 900-year-old guy (give or take 10 years) next door to him came out and asked the same thing. Same response.

Most weeks now my son and I mow seven yards in addition to the church. We spend time together every weekend and get to share a slushy for our hard work on the hotter days. He's learning to mow. He's learning to serve. He's growing comfortable saying, "You don't need to pay me. We just do this so you know Jesus loves you." And he's learning it with and from me.

Back on the financial side, all our kids enjoy helping count the cash and put it into envelopes on Budget Night. We have our budget built out and have withdrawn the right denominations from the bank. (This procedure is not included in this book, but email info@compass1.org and I'll show you my tricks.) Then it's just a matter of telling the child how many of what denomination go in which envelope. This gives them the opportunity to be a part of the process and has helped them start their own envelope system (more to come on that later).

We don't need their help, and we occasionally end up with an untraceable mistake resulting in too much or not enough bills to fill the envelopes, but it gets them excited to do their own budgeting and gets them involved in and used to the process.

GOD, OUR LEADER

Now, we turn back to Scripture to see providing practical opportunities in action. The first example we'll look at is found in the Gospel of Luke, beginning in chapter 8. Luke retells the stories of Jesus calming a storm, casting out a demon, healing a sick woman, and raising a dead girl back to life. He then turns to His disciples in chapter 9 and sends them out to do the same.

At this point in His ministry, He had healed many illnesses and cast out several demons. His companions had seen all this and heard His teachings about His Father, the kingdom of God, and the power of faith. So Jesus gives them an assignment with some additional instructions. They are to go out from village to village doing as they had been taught. Some unknown time later, Jesus sends 72 others to do the same. Clearly, Jesus didn't believe He would be solely responsible for advancing the gospel: He wanted to properly train the next generation of leaders for the tasks He was currently doing.

In each case, He chose assignments for His followers based on their preparation and skills, followed up with feedback and redirection, and celebrated their successes.

The next example is the broad application of Matthew 28:18-20. Notice Jesus' words, their progression, and their meaning.

- *"All authority in heaven and on earth has been given to me."* — I am now the rightful Ruler of this world.
- *"Therefore . . ."* — because I am now the rightful Ruler of this world . . .
- *"Go and make disciples of all nations, baptizing them in the name of the Father and of the Son and of the Holy Spirit, and teaching them to obey everything I have commanded you . . ."* — Under the authority that is mine, go do what I trained you to do.
- *"And surely I am with you always, to the very end of the age."* — I'm still here to help, challenge, and encourage you.

Isn't this exactly what we're trying to do as Christian parents? Build a base of knowledge and skills so our children can carry on the mission of our family and Christ? That's what Jesus' ministry was all about.

Although Jesus knew from the very beginning that he was going to die, He also knew He would have three years to train up a small group of faithful disciples to carry out His work and build His Church. He showed them what it looked like to commit to God. He told them all about the kingdom and how it was meant to operate. Then He gave them responsibility for executing the plan with His ongoing presence watching over them.

Robert Coleman, again in *Master Plan of Evangelism,* puts it this way (emphasis added):

> This was the way his church was to win—**through the dedicated lives of those who knew the Savior so well** that his Spirit and method constrained them to tell others. As simple as it may seem, this was the way the gospel would conquer. **He had no other plan.**

Our final example of God providing practical opportunities comes from creation itself. As we saw earlier, in the beginning, God created. He created the physical and the spiritual. He created light and dark. He created the water, land, and plants. He created the sun, moon, and stars. He created the birds and the fish. And He created the animals and us (Genesis 1:1-27). He was clearly in control with no contenders or threats to His throne.

But the next thing He did was unexpected from our earthly perspective. He put Adam and Eve in charge. He told them to go out into the world and to subdue it. He made them the overseers of everything on earth. Of the plants and animals, whether in the air, in the water, or on the ground (Genesis 1:28-30).

Along with this control, He also gave them training. He spent time with them, walking and talking. He gave them instructions about which trees were good and which one was bad. He gave them little assignments like naming the animals, eventually increasing their responsibility.

From the beginning, God has had a part and we have had a part. We *can't* do His and He *won't* do ours. He is the Creator and Sustainer but allows and requires us to be involved as well.

Jerry Bridges' book *Trusting God*[9] dedicates an entire chapter to the topic of God's Sovereignty and Our Responsibility. Here a few examples to firmly establish this point.

In Exodus, God hardened Pharoah's heart, but Moses and Aaron had to confront him.

In Esther, God could save Israel from Haman's plan, but Esther had to use her influence with King Xerxes.

In Daniel, God had promised to deliver Israel from exile, but someone had to pray for it after 70 years.

In Jonah, God had a plan to save Nineveh, but Jonah had to deliver the message.

In Acts, Jesus prepares Saul's conversion, but Ananias had to go heal him.

Later in Acts, God promises to spare every crew member of the ship transporting Paul, but only if they don't jump ship.

I could go on like this for a while. Over and over, we see that God prepares people for a task and then gives them the opportunity to use their knowledge and skills to accomplish it. We *can't* do His part and He *won't* do ours.

No doubt about it, this world would be a lot cleaner if God just did everything without our help. But He sees some value in our participation that we don't. We're being prepared for something, and from His perspective this is the best way to do it. We should do the same by preparing our children for their tasks—then allow and encourage them to practice what they've learned.

A WORD OF WARNING

As with the other two MVP components, there are a few things to keep in mind as we provide Practical Opportunities for our children. The first is to be prepared for them to make mistakes and be prepared to allow them to make them. No matter how small the task you give them, they will likely mess up the first few times. Be prepared and remember that this is a part of the learning process.

Jesus had to deal with His disciples constantly getting things wrong, but they eventually got it right and successfully built the Church in His name, to His honor, and for His glory.

Mistakes are an essential part of learning. The best time for your kids to make a mistake is when the tasks are small, the stakes are low, and you're around to help. Your reaction to their mistakes will make or break their willingness to try new things. If you flip out, they will not want to try the next task you give them. If you respond calmly and offer them the chance to fix their mistake or try again, they'll be more excited to try the next task you offer.

Even the way you respond to their mistakes is training them

how to respond to mistakes. If they see you flip out when you or others make mistakes, they're going to grow up flipping out when they or others (including you) make mistakes.

Second, be patient. Whatever you give them to do will take them at least three to four thousand times as long as it takes you. View it as an investment. You can keep $100,000 in your sock drawer and have immediate access to it all the time. Or, you can invest it and see growth, but it won't be accessible right away. Your kids are a worthwhile investment. If you're in a hurry and can't pragmatically be patient, explain to them that this task needs to be done quickly, but that they can watch you this time and help next time. Then make sure you let them help next time.

Finally, don't pawn off the terrible jobs just so you don't have to do them. We've all seen *Karate Kid*. (If you haven't, you probably should so you understand my reference.) As inspirational as the Mr. Miyagi method is, our kids won't get it when they're the ones sanding the floor and painting the fence for free because we're "training them for godliness."

Chores are extremely valuable for the development of character, work ethic, and self-worth, but our goal in assigning chores should be those that prepare them for the future and give them responsibility, not just whatever we don't want to do ourselves. If you wouldn't want to do the job yourself, consider paying them extra for their help.

Our oldest son wanted his own cell phone. We told him he could clean the bathrooms every week for ten dollars (in addition to his allowance). We absolutely offered him that particular job because we hate cleaning the bathrooms, but he knows exactly what he's getting out of the deal. Yes, we're building his work ethic and training him for the essential, though not glamorous, task of cleaning bathrooms as an adult. More than that, though, we're giving him the ability to earn something he wants. We know it and he knows it.

We make a point of always providing work for our children if they want to earn extra money. We won't give them money (aside from their allowance), and we won't loan them money, but we will provide a job they can do to earn the money.

One last time, here are the same Goals with questions to help you start thinking about what you want for your children and how you can provide Practical Opportunities for them to practice.

- What do my children need to know about work and income to be faithful followers of Jesus and how can I provide them opportunities to practice what I've taught them?
- What do my children need to know about giving and spending to be faithful followers of Jesus and how can I provide them opportunities to practice what I've taught them?
- What do my children need to know about planning and budgeting to be faithful followers of Jesus and how can I provide them opportunities to practice what I've taught them?
- What do my children need to know about executing a financial plan to be faithful followers of Jesus and how can I provide them opportunities to practice what I've taught them?
- What do my children need to know about accounting for their finances to be faithful followers of Jesus and how can I provide them opportunities to practice what I've taught them?

THREE BIGGEST TAKEAWAYS FROM THIS CHAPTER

1)

2)

3)

PART 3

Financial Discipleship in Our Parenting

CHAPTER 8

Financial Discipleship

*"Come, follow me," Jesus said, "and I will
send you out to fish for people."*

MATTHEW 4:19

So what is a "financial disciple" anyway? We've talked all around it and we're seven chapters deep in a book about it, but as we get to the brass tacks of financially discipling our children, we should get the matter straight.

Let's start with what a disciple is. Most of us have heard the term around church, especially as it relates to the twelve disciples, but we could stand to know more of what it entails before we sign our kids up.

A disciple is a follower, a student, a trainee. In Jesus' day, a disciple was a person fully committed to learning a skill or trade. Jesus' disciples lived with Him, traveled with Him, learned from Him, and emulated Him. Their task, when Jesus said, "Follow me," was clear to them. If they accepted His invitation, their goal was to learn to be like Jesus in every way.

This wasn't a call to friendship, employment, or a small-group study. It was a total commitment for as long as it took. The expectation was that His disciples would learn, apply, and multiply everything He did and instructed. As we saw in our chapter on

Practical Opportunities, this was Jesus' plan for establishing and growing His Church. There was no plan B.

A financial disciple, then, is simply a person who learns, applies, and multiplies the Bible's teachings about money and possessions. They learn what the Bible says about money and possessions, apply it to their lives, and multiply it into the lives of others.

The Church today has rediscovered the importance of discipleship, thanks in large part to the previously mentioned Robert Coleman, but it's tough to replicate Jesus-style discipleship in today's society.

I'm part of a discipleship program with Compass-finances God's way in which I've committed to "discipling" at least one person every year. We agree to read a series of incredibly impactful books, meet to discuss their significance, build relationships and friendships, and equip them to do the same. It's had a profound impact on my life and the lives of over 100 people who have been part of the program in just the past few years. Even so, this experience and impact falls short of what Jesus did with His disciples.

I recall a deep conversation with one of the men I discipled about how I could actually disciple him like Jesus did. What would it take? Would he and his family have to move in with my family? Would he need to shadow me at work? Would he just follow me around all the time taking notes? We concluded that replicating what Jesus' disciples went through would be nearly impossible in our culture. Although it might not be entirely impossible, it would certainly be a few degrees beyond impractical. It made a lot more sense in an apprenticeship-based society where the process would have been understood, accepted, and even expected.

Today it would be extremely difficult and disruptive. Unless, of course, your disciple was already spending nearly all their time with you—in your home, in your car, eating all your food—essentially woven into the fabric of your life. Realistically, the closest we can ever get to Jesus-style discipleship is with our family, our spouse and kids. It's in this environment that Jesus-style discipleship is most natural and offers the greatest impact on those following us.

The concept of financial discipleship is built on five foundational pillars: Ownership, Surrender, Choice, Multiplication, and Eternal Focus. I'll briefly introduce and establish each here but will go into much greater detail over the next five chapters.

OWNERSHIP

The Bible is clear that God owns it all. We can see it plainly in verses like Psalm 89:11, *"The heavens are yours, and yours also the earth; you founded the world and all that is in it,"* and 1 Chronicles 29:11, *". . . for everything in heaven and earth is yours. Yours, Lord, is the kingdom . . . ,"* and less plainly in many other places.

Although God entrusts "our possessions" to us, He never surrenders ownership. We see this demonstrated in the parable of the talents found in Matthew 25:14-30. We hear that the gold belongs to the master at the start of the story. He entrusts it to his servants for a while, then calls them back to give an account of their investments. We often think the gold was *given* to the servants or even that keeping it is their reward, but what we actually read here is that the gold is returned to the master. He remains the owner even as he rewards the faithful servants with additional responsibility for more of his property.

The same is true for us. Everything we have belongs to God but has been entrusted to our care for a short time. One day, we'll return it all and account for how we used it for His glory. A clear understanding of God's ownership should immediately humble us and fundamentally change our perspective on how we manage "our" finances, since it's actually God's finances we're managing (No pressure . . .).

SURRENDER

Once we recognize God's ownership of all "our" possessions, we must surrender them to Him through our actions. In Luke 14:33, Jesus says, *"In the same way, those of you who do not give up everything you have cannot be my disciples."*

True surrender requires us to inwardly and outwardly return all we thought we owned (our stuff, our families, our life) back to its true owner. While He will likely keep it in our custody, we must willingly recognize it is His to give or take away. This is a difficult step but also incredibly freeing, enabling us to let the worry and anxiety that plagues us to fall instead on God's much more capable shoulders. We are still responsible for our part but not the rest. We can be confident that God will do His part.

Looking back at past wars and conflicts, we often hear about the "conditional surrender" of one side or the other. They will concede the battle as long as some set of criteria is met. This is *not* the kind of surrender Jesus requires. Jesus owns it all and wants us to surrender it all. And while this has implications in every area of our life, it's often most difficult to fully surrender our finances to God. Difficult as it may be, though, it's essential to establishing a healthier relationship with Him through a healthier relationship with money and possessions.

As Howard Dayton puts it, surrendering our finances to God will turn every spending decision into a spiritual decision. Instead of asking ourselves what we should do with *our* money, we will ask God what He would like us to do with *His* money.

CHOICE

The third pillar focuses on the day-by-day, moment-by-moment choice between two masters. As Jesus puts it in Matthew 6:24, *"No one can serve two masters. Either you will hate the one and love the other, or you will be devoted to the one and despise the other. You cannot serve both God and money."*

Please notice that although there are many different opposing "masters" Jesus could have included, He chose one and only one in this statement: money. This passage is embedded in the Sermon on the Mount, where Jesus goes from topic to topic covering all sorts of virtues and temptations. In all of these, there is only one where He makes such a decisive contrast, "you cannot serve both God and _____": it is applied only to money. Jesus is pointing out the unique nature of money in its false offer of independence and its opposition to the one true path.

Greg Gilbert in his book *What is the Gospel?*[10] makes the point that many are quick to accept Jesus as their Savior but resist making Him their Lord. If He is our King and we are His people, He must be both. He will save us, but we must accept His leadership of our lives and our finances. In every decision we make, large or small, we must choose God's path over the tempting independence and self-reliance money appears to offer.

Will we worship the Creator or the created? Will we invest in God's economy or the world's? Will our reward be eternal or temporary? We get to choose, but we *must* choose. If we choose God, we must choose Him over and over with every financial decision we make.

MULTIPLICATION

Now that our own house is in order, we must push past stewardship and shift our focus to multiplying the growth of God's kingdom. As disciples of Jesus, we are clearly and repeatedly instructed to multiply. Whether using money, time, talents, knowledge, or anything else God has entrusted to us, we are expected to use it to grow God's kingdom.

In John 1:41, we read that the first thing Andrew did after meeting Jesus was to tell his brother Simon. The parable of the minas in Luke 19:11-27 teaches us that when the Master entrusts us with something, He expects it returned with growth. In the Matthew 13 parable of the sower, the only soil considered *"good"* was the one that multiplied.

The Great Commission, Jesus' final instruction before ascending to heaven, is all about multiplication. *"Go and make disciples... teaching them to obey everything I have commanded you"* (Matthew 28:18-20).

There has been a tremendous movement toward financial responsibility and stewardship in the Church over the past decade—and that is a good thing—but it doesn't fulfill the calling of Christ. If we are to be true disciples of Jesus: going where He goes, doing what He does, and becoming like He is, it requires multiplication. Each step we take in our journeys of faith must be learned, applied, and multiplied for maximum kingdom impact.

ETERNAL FOCUS

The final foundational pillar of financial discipleship overarches the other four. As disciples of Christ, we must always stay focused on the *eternal* outcomes of our choices rather than the temporary outcomes this world tries to distract us with.

In Matthew 6:19-20 Jesus tells us not to put our hope in treasures on earth, *"where moths and vermin destroy, and where thieves break in and steal,"* but to store up treasures in heaven, where they are safe forever.

He then gives us valuable insight into human nature in verse 21 by adding, *"where your treasure is, there your heart will be also."* If you pause for a moment to think about this, it will likely seem contradictory to your expectations. Most of us would be quick to admit that we spend money on the things we enjoy, but this verse tells us we will enjoy most the things we spend money on. The location of our treasure is going to be a big factor in where our hearts go, and if we continually keep our focus on treasures in heaven, our heart will follow, even when our brains may not want to.

An eternal focus drives us to consider the kingdom impact rather than the temporary impact of our spending decisions. We may still occasionally choose to buy the fountain drink at the gas station or the five-dollar latte at the coffee shop, but it will be because it brings us joy and is an expression of our thankfulness to God rather than a thoughtless splurge. It will likely mean that we limit those purchases, though, as we consider alternative uses for that money and instead opt to invest in ones that will bring more glory to God and lead to greater growth of His kingdom. Either way we choose, we will stay focused on the eternal impact of our choices rather than the temporary.

APPLYING FINANCIAL DISCIPLESHIP TO OUR FAMILIES

The next five chapters weave together the various elements of marriage, parenting, and finances to help us develop our own plans for discipling our children in the area of money and possessions. As we've said before, it first requires us to learn and apply biblical financial principles that we can then multiply in the lives of others (our children). We must Model them ourselves, be prepared to explain them through Verbal Instruction, and give our children Practical Opportunities to do them themselves. We strive to do all of this in a way that's active rather than reactive, embracing our influence rather than control.

Because children have simple financial lives with very limited income and expenses, budgets (ours and theirs) will be the centerpieces of our structure. We'll get our budgets right by applying the five pillars of financial discipleship, which we Model as consistently as possible. We'll have the necessary theological and practical background knowledge to give them Verbal Instruction. We'll encourage, enable, and require them to follow suit as we provide Practical Opportunities.

We hope to present this clearly enough that we will be able to closely replicate our own financial plan and execution with our kids. They'll have income, expenses, and a plan. They'll be confronted with situations that require them to weigh the benefits of opposing alternatives and have the freedom to choose. They'll have to account for those choices in real time in order to evolve and adapt their plan in the future. They'll experience the benefits of good decisions and the pain of poor ones. And they'll do it all with our guidance and instruction.

IMPLICATIONS OF FINANCIAL DISCIPLESHIP FOR YOUR FAMILY

Before launching into our application, I want to invest a few more pages in some extremely important preparation. First, one final reminder of what's at stake and why we should go through all the effort of developing and implementing a financial discipleship plan for our families.

The next five chapters will seem like a lot. Some long and packed, with lots to think about.

Transformational changes to our own lives.

A ton of time and effort being poured into our marriages and our kids' lives, and therefore a lot of time not doing some other things we enjoy.

At times, it may seem like what I'm advocating for is total surrender. It is. Total, complete, and unconditional surrender. Not to this book, its methods, or financial discipleship on the whole, but to Jesus. To being the spouse and parent we've been called to be. For His glory and our good.

The task ahead of us may seem monumental, but as you'll see, it's absolutely worth it. There are five key benefits, and they're big.

A Closer Relationship with God

First and foremost, financial discipleship with our families will draw each individual and the family as a whole into a closer relationship with God. As we learn and apply God's teaching in preparation to multiply it in the lives of our children, we will find ourselves spending more time studying Scripture and in prayer.

As we provide Modeling, Verbal Instruction, and Practical Opportunities through our five pillars of financial discipleship, our kids will likewise learn to become reliant on Scripture and prayer in their own lives. Too often we, and therefore our children, treat the Bible as a book of great ideas and ideals. And prayer becomes all about thanking God for our food and asking for Aunt Sally's bunion to stop hurting.

The Bible and prayer should be much, much more than that. The Bible should be viewed as a book of both description and prescription, a book that describes what God has made and instructs us how to best live in it. A book not just to be read, or even to be studied, but a book to be read, studied, and obeyed.

A healthy prayer life will certainly include thanking God for our food and relief of bunion pain. But more importantly it's a time of true fellowship and communion with the Creator of everything, enabling us to tell Him what's on our mind and hear what's on His.

When we, in plain view of our spouse and children, open God's word and seek His direct input on everyday financial questions through prayer, we model our full reliance on God's wisdom. As we explain our decisions to our children, they learn not only what we've told them but also the importance of Scripture and prayer in a healthy adult's life. They develop a baseline that God's word and His Spirit's influence are the primary, if not only, criteria to consider in any decision, financial or otherwise. And as they make their own financial plans and decisions, they will naturally follow our lead, resulting in a stronger relationship with God, and at a much younger age.

The prerequisite of this closer relationship, of course, is the surrender of their finances to God. Learning to humbly seek God's wisdom through Scripture and prayer requires surrender. It requires us and them to *". . . lean not on your own understanding; in all your ways submit to Him . . ."* (Proverbs 3:5-6).

Even more than God wants us to obey Him, He wants us to humble ourselves before Him. As seen in the parable of the Pharisee and the tax collector in Luke 18, humility before God offers greater kingdom value than does adherence to the law. As we and our children defer financial decisions to God, we confess our shortcomings and inability to determine good from bad, demonstrate our utter dependence on Him, and allow ourselves the opportunity to be exalted by Him (Matthew 23:12).

A Closer Relationship with Us

The second major outcome of developing and implementing a financial discipleship plan for your family is that you will experience closer relationships with your family members. The first reason for this is simply because you will be spending more time together. No, this isn't going to be a ten-hour-per-week endeavor, but it'll be something. Distributing income, developing and modifying budgets, and talking through past, present, and future spending decisions gives you new reasons to be together.

My friend who's a little further along in life and parenting warns me often that as my kids grow up, they will want to spend less and less time with me. With his kids now in their upper-teenage years, he does his best to be part of what they're doing, but he recognizes that he's pursuing the relationship more now than they are. Creating a cadence of getting together builds a structure to fall back on. And even if the cadence doesn't survive the teenage years, the time spent together in their younger years will be time you (and hopefully they) will cherish later.

Just as importantly, this time together and shared experience creates an alignment of values and a shared vision for your family.

Most of my extended family members are not Christians (yet).

Because of that, they think we're crazy to have paid off our house at a time when interest rates were 3.5 percent and the stock market was growing 15+ percent a year. They were thinking here and now; we were thinking there (heaven) and forever.

Ignoring the eventual market collapse, we were doing what God said, *"Let no debt remain outstanding, except the continuing debt to love one another . . ."* (Romans 13:8) and trusting His wisdom over our own.

Unfortunately, until those family members come to Christ, they won't get it. Erica and our kids, however, do. They understand the immediate financial implications but know that we'll trust God's math over man's every time. They may someday adopt a worldly perspective about "good and bad debt," but they will always have the baseline experience that God says no debt is good, so we, as a family, chose to eliminate it.

As we have discussions with our children about our financial plans and theirs, they will be confronted and influenced by our commitment to live simply and contently. Later in life, they'll have to make their own choices on the matter, but for now they understand why we choose to live like we do. They may want the new and most expensive thing, but during their time with us they'll witness the intrinsic benefits of a life with minimal "stuff."

Greater Contentment in Life

Similarly, helping our families learn and apply God's financial principles also leads to greater contentment in their lives. Paul teaches us in Philippian 4:11-13 that contentment is something we *learn*, not something our sinful nature offers freely. By following God's instruction, we become increasingly reliant on Him for our life's vision and provision and more accurately reflect Jesus' character. Our relationship with Jesus deepens and, like Jesus, we are increasingly able to distinguish our needs from our wants and naturally experience greater freedom from the materialistic desires our sinful nature prefers.

As we and our children learn to be content in all circumstances, it will be both a result and a cause: a result of aligning our priorities to God's and an ongoing cause of even greater alignment. When we value what God values, dismiss what God dismisses, and store up our treasures in the eternal reality rather than the temporary, we more vividly recognize the gifts and grace God has given us.

In turn, because we see what He's doing in our lives, we develop greater trust and confidence in His provision, experiencing more consistent contentment. If one of our ultimate goals for our children is for them to be Christ-like adults, the contentment they learn through our Modeling, Verbal Instruction, and Practical Opportunities is an essential and invaluable step in the process.

As a side benefit, contentment is also likely to lead to greater financial stability for us and our children. As we saw with the Proverbs, God's financial instructions are not promised to lead to wealth, but the consistent practice of being content with what we have is likely to lead to lower expenses and consumption, greater generosity, and an attitude of "steady plodding" that leads to financial stability in the long run.

When we are discontent with what we have, we build the habit of consistently buying more, newer, and better stuff. When we buy stuff, it costs money to have, store, use, repair, or replace it. Once we have something for a while, it stops being a "nice-to-have" and becomes a "must-have," meaning when it fails (or just gets too old or out of style), we feel the need to replace it rather than just do without it.

We get into this cycle as an outward expression of an inner discontentment, believing what we have isn't sufficient or good enough. As we train our children to be content in all circumstances, they avoid this financially costly cycle of consumerism. It also helps them apply the steady plodding principle that results in greater long-term stability from both an income and expense perspective.

Increased Kingdom Productivity

As we and our children focus on the eternal rather than the temporary, we also experience greater productivity for the kingdom. As I personally align my life, finances, and priorities to God's, I have to make choices on where I'll spend my limited time and money. Focusing on what creates the greatest kingdom impact, as discerned from Scripture and through prayer, I choose to spend my time, efforts, and money on the things that mean the most to God (and therefore not on the things that don't).

As we said earlier, active parenting is a lot of work. Financially discipling your children, once you get into the swing of things, will only take a few hours a month. But applying MVP Parenting to every aspect of your parenting will make training your kids a full-time job.

I love bowling and used to be pretty good at it, but I don't join the bowling league because my job, ministry, and family are greater priorities. I used to enjoy golfing, though I was not very good, but have put it aside for the same reason. I used to enjoy watching football, but my wife and kids don't, so I have to choose whether to spend time with them or the Fightin' Irish. And all of these hobbies can get expensive, meaning they consume the limited money I have and leave less for generous giving, family activities, or college savings.

As my children grow up with their priorities more closely aligned to God's, they will find it easier to align their activities and spending as well. They are more likely to truly enjoy doing God's work, studying His word, and giving generously to His causes. They will spend significantly more time and money on the meaningful and significantly less time and money on the meaningless. My children, with a 30-year head start, will be able to accomplish so much more for God than I will, simply because they had greater focus at an earlier age.

Leaving a Legacy

Finally, as we disciple our families, we build an incredibly God-glorifying legacy for generations to come. Back to the principle of "steady plodding" mentioned before. In Proverbs 21:5, we are told that *"The plans of the diligent lead to profit as surely as haste leads to poverty."* Howard describes this diligence or "steady plodding" as filling a barrel one handful at a time. Each scoop adds relatively little to the total, but with patience and persistence, the barrel is filled.

Imagine if you made the simple commitment today that you

would be a better, more God-focused parent to your children than your parents were to you. What if your children made the same commitment? And theirs? It wouldn't take long before this world would be a much better place.

We can't control the commitment our kids make, but we can make the commitment ourselves and do our best to start a generational cycle of Christ-like parenting.

As we learn, apply, and multiply God's financial principles through the application of the five pillars and MVP Parenting, we will be training our children to do the same. As they do the same with their children (with our assistance and support as grandparents), we will leave a legacy that grows from generation to generation. As each generation learns, applies, and multiplies God's financial principles within their own family, the baseline of honoring God with our finances becomes stronger and stronger and more and more natural.

THREE BIGGEST TAKEAWAYS FROM THIS CHAPTER

1)

2)

3)

CHAPTER 9

Ownership

Yours, Lord, is the greatness and the power and the glory and the majesty and the splendor, for everything in heaven and earth is yours. Yours, Lord, is the kingdom; you are exalted as head over all. Wealth and honor come from you; you are the ruler of all things. In your hands are strength and power to exalt and give strength to all.

1 CHRONICLES 29:11-12

As we learned in the brief overview of Ownership in Chapter 8, God owns it all. He's entrusted the care of many things to us, allowing us to be part of His creation and the work He is doing. He expects us to do our part while trusting Him to do His, but He never transfers ownership to us.

There are two sides of this that have a significant impact on our financial discipleship journey and how we teach and train our children. The first is that everything we have is a gift from God. God has given you more than just the first ten percent of your income: He's provided it all. He's given you your job, your car, your home, your lawnmower, and your family. Even though they may not be ideal from your perspective, they are exactly what God intended you to have. We should be quick to recognize God's gifts to us even when they seem small, insignificant, or less than ideal.

The other side is that if it's all God's, none of it is ours. He's loaned us these tools to help us grow into His own image, to help us be holy because He is holy (Leviticus 19:2). To help us spread His salvation and build His kingdom.

We are called not only to care for and protect all that He has entrusted to us but also to be *"faithful stewards"* (1 Peter 4:10), using these gifts to fulfill *His* purposes rather than our own. When we stand before His throne to give an account for all that we did with His stuff, the last thing He's going to want to hear about is how we accomplished *our* goals. If we and our children are going to be judged *"good and faithful servants,"* we need to be focusing on accomplishing *His* goals (Matthew 25:21).

For our family to create financial plans that help us develop a stronger relationship with God, we first need to understand His five priorities for how we spend money. God didn't give us a force-ranked list in Scripture, but I present them here in the order I believe is consistent with Scripture. After defending my position and reasoning, I leave you, your spouse, and the Spirit to decide if reordering them for your family is appropriate.

In Chapter 10, we will begin applying these priorities as we make a budget for ourselves and help our children make theirs. We'll apply them with a continual focus on our MVP mindset, providing Modeling, Verbal Instruction, and Practical Opportunities for each. Although this mindset is new and exciting, it's not yet second nature, so we frequently remind ourselves of it until it is.

PRIORITY 1: GIVING GENEROUSLY

God's first priority for our finances is to give generously back to Him and His work. A few of the *many* verses that defend this as God's top priority are:

Exodus 34:26a— *"Bring the best of the firstfruits of your soil to the house of the Lord your God."* This stresses the importance of giving the first and the best to God. If any other financial priority were to come before this, it would make it impossible to offer God both the first and the best of our income.

2 Corinthians 9:7—*"Each of you should give what you have decided in your heart to give, not reluctantly or under compulsion, for God loves a cheerful giver."* This shows how giving should align our heart to God and demonstrate an attitude that reflects the fruit of the Spirit, especially joy.

Psalm 37:21—*"The wicked borrow and do not repay, but the righteous give generously."* This associates righteousness with generosity. We are called to be holy because He is holy; being generous as He is generous is the best place to start.

Although I believe these three verses alone make a great case for giving's supreme importance in God's priorities for money, it's also noteworthy to recognize the sheer volume of God's communication on this topic. By Compass's count, there are nearly 300 passages in Scripture relating to and offering instruction on the topic of giving. (You can find the full list at https://compass1.org/2350-verses.)

To be clear, the number of times something appears in Scripture doesn't directly communicate its importance and kingdom value. If something is included once in Scripture, it's authoritative and important. God shouldn't have to repeat Himself for us to pay attention any more than we want to have to do it with *our* children. But when He offers us nearly 300 pieces of insight on a specific topic, it should certainly communicate both its importance and our tendency to need a nudge from time to time (or all the time).

Benefits of Giving Generously
We get to honor God. As we see in 1 Chronicles 29:10-13, God, the owner of everything, is also the supreme giver. We should see giving as an opportunity to be like Him. Our gratitude for all He has given us begs for practical expression of our love and appreciation back to Him.

It's like when our kids give us gifts. Somewhere up the line, the money came from us. Whether they used allowance money or our spouse took them to the store and paid for it, the money used for the gift was probably ours to start with. But it still has incredible meaning to us that they wanted to buy us something, especially when they could easily have chosen to buy something for themselves instead. We have the same opportunity with God. The money is His anyway, but He allows us the freedom to do what we want with it. Wanting to make Him our first priority reflects our genuine appreciation for His gifts.

We get to impact the kingdom. Acts 4:34-35 demonstrates this well as the early Church members sold property to provide for the needs of their fellow believers. Like our children "helping" us fix the lawnmower or cook dinner even though we could do it ourselves, the act of helping God with His work builds a stronger relationship with Him as it makes us more like Christ. Could God have met the needs of those early Church members Himself? Absolutely. But He invited the Church to care for one another. And they, the givers, greatly benefited from their own generosity. We have the same opportunity with our giving.

We grow to love God's kingdom more. Jesus put it succinctly in Matthew 6:21, *"For where your treasure is, there your heart will be also."* As we give generously to God's work, we come to love it more and more, to be more invested in its growth and more passionate about its success. When we give to specific causes, we naturally find ourselves more interested in the work they are doing, spending more time in prayer for them, and even reading the prayer letters they send out periodically.

We break the emotional hold of materialism. Matthew 19:16-24 tells the story of a wealthy young man who wanted to attain eternal life. He was a good man who had followed the commandments his whole life, even by Jesus' standard! All he had to do to gain eternal life, according to Jesus, was to sell all his possessions, give them to the poor, and follow Him. He couldn't do it.

Most of us think we would have chosen differently, but let's give it a try. Think about selling your home and giving the proceeds to a local church or mission. Think about the impact it could have on the kingdom: the good it could do for the poor and the lost, the people who could be brought into a relationship with Jesus. But also think about the money you'd be giving up and where you'd live. Think about all the money and work you've put into the house. Think about the complexity of finding a new house without a down payment and having to pack your stuff and actually move.

Do you feel that? It's halfway between your head exploding and throwing up your vital organs (or maybe both). That's probably the same feeling the rich young man had, and I didn't even ask you to sell *everything* and quit your job, which is what Jesus required of him!

When we give, we chip a corner off the stumbling block that obstructs our path to holiness. The next time we give, we knock another corner off. By creating a habit of generosity, we little by little sand that block of fear and insecurity down to a fine dust and remove its power over us.

We grow in faith of God's provision. After freeing the Israelites from Egypt and decimating Pharoah's army in the Red Sea, God gives some very specific instructions in Exodus 16. They are to collect one day's worth of manna each morning for five days, then a double portion on the sixth day, and none on the seventh. Any extra collected on days one through five would rot, but not on day six. God was proving a point here. He can provide. Even through difficult times and by miraculous means, He can provide.

Later, God challenges the Israelites in their giving when He says through Malachi, *"'Bring the whole tithe into the storehouse, that there may be food in my house. Test me in this,' says the LORD Almighty, 'and see if I will not throw open the floodgates of heaven and pour out so much blessing that there will not be room enough to store it'"* (Malachi 3:10). God has promised to provide for us and has instructed us to give generously. As we follow His instructions, we get to see more clearly His divine provision. When we don't give generously, it becomes easy to rely on ourselves rather than God.

We model this priority for our children by both giving generously and making them aware of it. Little things like hanging the pictures of the kids we sponsor on the refrigerator elicit questions from them and give us the opportunity to explain why we give. Erica and I require our children to tithe, and we encourage additional giving when opportunities arise.

PRIORITY 2: PROVIDING FOR THE NEEDS OF YOUR FAMILY

The defense of this second priority is much more straightforward. In 1 Timothy 5:8, Paul says, *"Anyone who does not provide for their relatives, and especially for their own household, has denied the faith and is worse than an unbeliever."* So, anyone want to argue this one? Or claim, "taken out of context?" Didn't think so.

All joking aside, while this single verse makes clear the importance of providing for the needs of our families, it leaves it pretty wide open as to who is included in our households and what provisions are in play. Paul's recognition that *"relatives"* are different from *"household"* is noteworthy. Paul is saying that meeting the needs of our household (our spouse and children) is primary. Supporting parents and siblings who are unable to support themselves is secondary, though still important.

As to what is in play, I look at it as the essential level of food, shelter, and clothing to sustain a reasonable life. There are certainly foods, shelters, and clothing which are above and beyond the needs of a person, but I believe Paul is speaking to the needs portion rather than the wants portion. As we move further down our priorities, we may have the opportunity to upgrade from needs to wants, but the priority now is just the needs. For example, buying groceries is a need; eating out is not. Having a home is a need; everyone having their own bedroom is not. Having shoes is a need; having name-brand shoes is not.

Most children young or old won't have many, if any, expenses tied to this priority. If your teenager has a job and you and your spouse believe they should help with some bills, those would go here. Even if they don't have any line items like this, there's a lot of value in talking about this stuff with them. It helps them gain some perspective on how much life costs.

I remember as a kid thinking $100 was the ultimate amount of money. Little did I know it wouldn't even cover my electric bill in college. I wish I could say talking about all this made our kids stop asking us to spend all our money on trampoline parks, fast food, and inground pools with 12 waterslides and water-shooting jets.

But still, we can see their little brains turning when we talk to them about this stuff, so we're guessing it would be worse if we didn't.

PRIORITY 3: MEETING YOUR FINANCIAL OBLIGATIONS

Romans 13:7-8 teaches, *"Give to everyone what you owe them: If you owe taxes, pay taxes; if revenue, then revenue; if respect, then respect; if honor, then honor. Let no debt remain outstanding, except for the continuing debt to love one another, for whoever loves others has fulfilled the law."* After giving and providing for the basic needs of our family, we need to prioritize meeting the various financial obligations we have made. This may include paying taxes, meeting contractual obligations, and repaying any outstanding debt we have.

As we work to get our finances aligned to God's priorities, most of us will find that some of our debt and contractual obligations fit more into Priority 5—Enjoying God's Abundant Blessing rather than Priority 2—Meeting the Needs of our Family.

Jesus advises us in Matthew 5:34 to avoid unnecessary obligations, but once we've made them, the honoring of our commitment becomes imperative, as established in Romans 13:7-8. From Jesus' perspective, it would be best if we could avoid having these altogether, but if that ship has sailed, we must fulfill our obligations and avoid making new ones.

As important as keeping our commitments is, I still believe this priority falls behind Giving, because of the sheer abundance of God's instruction on giving. It falls behind Providing for our Family because of the harsh verdict if we don't.

Younger children probably won't have any financial commitments, but they will as they get older. Cell phone plans are a good example. If they are signed up for a long-term contract (as opposed to month-to-month service), they need to understand that their commitment is binding. Same thing if your children are responsible for paying for or contributing to things like car insurance or registration. Once they've made that commitment, it's binding. Come heck or high water, they're going to pay the bill because as Christians our yes means yes and our no means no (Matthew 5:37).

In most cases, we shouldn't allow our kids to borrow money—from us or anyone else. If they find themselves in a position where they've made a commitment (financial or otherwise), we need to encourage and require them to keep their commitment before any freedom to use their money for fun (Priority 5).

PRIORITY 4: SAVING FOR THE FUTURE

The simplest reason to make saving for the future a priority is that it allows us to continue giving generously, providing for our families, and meeting our obligations in times of financial hardship.

In Genesis 41:53-57, we read how Joseph followed God's instructions by saving up the abundance of seven years in order to survive the seven years of famine. In doing so, he saved Egypt, his relatives, and many others from starvation—all while giving the glory to God!

This is exactly how savings should work for us and our children. Whether it's Emergency Savings, College Savings, Retirement Savings, or just saving for a vacation, the premise is the same. We store up surplus now so that we can do what we've been called to do even when our income is disrupted.

An important question your kids will likely ask (and that you should also be asking yourself) is, "What am I saving for?" Too often, we adults just "save" because that's the wise thing to do (Proverbs 21:20). That's certainly better than not saving, but giving even your savings a specific purpose is extremely valuable. Is the extra money in the budget going to Emergency Savings, New Car Savings, or Vacation Savings? Clearly specifying its purpose helps ensure you don't end up using what should have been Emergency Savings for a vacation and not have adequate savings when an emergency happens.

Assigning our savings a purpose also helps us set God-centered financial "finish lines." Believe it or not, there is such a thing as saving too much. Saving too much occurs when our goals aren't aligned to God's or when we haven't "counted the cost."

This was actually my idol a few years ago. I've always been a saver. I *learned* to be generous, but saving always *came naturally*. At the end of each year, Erica and I look back at our monthly budgets and start to plan out next year. During this exercise, I was convicted that the biggest monthly expense on our budget was Retirement Savings. Bigger than giving. Bigger than the house payment. Bigger than anything else. So I dug in and asked why. Well, it was because I wanted to retire at 50. We'll talk more about retirement later, but this wasn't the kind of retirement where I go work for a nonprofit for minimal or no pay, which is consistent with biblical retirement. This was the kind of retirement where I sit around and eat ice cream between rounds of golf. Clearly, this isn't biblical.

For me, this kind of retirement was about comfort rather than Christ and aligned to *my* goals rather than God's. So I did some checking and made some new commitments. I could base my Retirement Savings on earning income until I was 67. I could assume a very conservative rate of growth and plan to maintain our current reasonably comfortable lifestyle. With these simple tweaks, we already had enough Retirement Savings! Even accounting for sending four kids to college, we had enough. Even after the fall and winter of 2022—one of the worst years in stock market history—we're still in good shape.

No doubt about it, I was over-saving. Once I set a finish line for our Retirement Savings and made the adjustment, it opened the opportunity to pay off our mortgage in record time. It allowed us to give generously to God's work. And it even encouraged us to put a little more into college funds and Emergency Savings as we realized we had under-saved for those.

Saving is a good thing as long as it aligns with God's purposes and plans. But it can't do that if it doesn't even have a purpose. If it's just left-over money, it isn't aligned with God's purpose. We need to be putting it all to use for God's kingdom.

Determine *what* you need to save for in order to fulfill God's purposes. Determine *how much* you need to save, and then get to work. When you reach the finish line, shift your efforts to God's next calling.

The same applies to our children. They are *required* to save for their future emergency fund and college expenses but are *encouraged* to save for things they want to buy. We also try to motivate them to save above and beyond the minimum required by offering them an annual match. My parents came up with this idea and I liked it so much I carried on the tradition. At the end of every year, whatever our kids have saved throughout the year for long-term savings, we match. So if they saved $100, we add another $100. If they only saved $52, we add another $52. It hasn't turned our spender into a saver, but it gets his attention when we remind him of it.

PRIORITY 5: ENJOYING GOD'S ABUNDANT BLESSINGS

God's final priority for money is for the enjoyment of His abundant blessings. We read in 1 Chronicles 29:28 that David dies, *"having enjoyed long life, wealth and honor."* Too often, we fluctuate from one extreme perspective to another regarding wealth.

We usually start by ignoring the topic, embracing wealth, and enjoying God's provision without due diligence on the more important priorities. Then one day, we read about the rich young man in Matthew 19 and the first half of Jesus' explanation that *"it is easier for a camel to go through the eye of a needle than for someone who is rich to enter the kingdom of God."* Or we hear the misquote of 1 Timothy 6:10 stating that, "money is the root of all evil," and come to the conclusion that poverty is the only way in.

Note, however, that Jesus finishes His statement about the wealthy getting into the kingdom by clarifying that, *"With man this is impossible, but with God all things are possible."* And 1 Timothy 6:10 *actually* says, *"The **love of** money is **a** root of all kinds of evil"* (emphasis added). It's not the wealth and abundance that is the problem: it's our choice of money over God.

In fact, abundant wealth can be an abundant blessing to the kingdom when it's put in the right hands. In John Rinehart's book *Gospel Patrons*,[11] he walks through the historical importance of individuals who used their wealth to advance the gospel of Jesus Christ.

We at Compass-finances God's way know this truth firsthand. Ninety percent of our funding comes from donations and a large portion of that comes from a small handful of Gospel Patrons. God has blessed them with amazing wealth, and they use it well. They invest in kingdom growth ahead of their own, storing up their treasures where moths don't destroy and rust won't corrode. They go on vacations, but they do it with what's left after God's higher priorities. They own second homes nicer than my first home but not until it's all been committed to the Lord. They don't flaunt their wealth, but they aren't ashamed of it either. God has provided it, and He's provided it for a purpose. He may not ever give me that kind of wealth, but I'll do what I can with what He *does* give.

If you've given generously, provided for your family and relatives, fulfilled all your financial obligations, and saved so that you can continue in time of hardship, God wants you to enjoy the abundance He's provided. Our part is to put first things first and enjoy His abundance, as much or as little as it might be, with sincere appreciation. The greater error is that we usually fulfill our wants ahead of our needs.

Our natural tendency is to order priorities a little more like this:

2. Providing for the Needs of Our Family
5. Enjoying God's Abundant Blessing
3. Meeting Our Financial Obligations
4. Saving for the Future
1. Giving the Leftovers (if there are any) to God

Erica and I are open with our children about why we can or cannot afford to do or buy some things. Simple responses like, "That would be great, but it'll have to wait for next month because we've had some unexpected expenses this month," or "Great idea, Curly Kid! (the superhero name of kid #3 who has curly hair). God gave us a little extra this month so it must have been for ice cream! Go tell the others and I'll get Mom. Last one in the van has to order vanilla!"

For their spending decisions, we want to encourage them to buy things they enjoy while ensuring they've put the first things first. We require them to give and save, and we still allow them to spend. The things they buy aren't always what I would want them to buy. But if a pack of Pokémon cards brings kid #2 joy and he's already given generously, saved for the future, and fulfilled his commitments, so be it. We're quick to remind him of the other things he said he wanted to buy, but ultimately let him choose what to do with the extra.

CLOSING THOUGHTS

To bring this chapter to a close, I want to remind us where we started. It's all God's. All of it. None of it is ours. If it were ours, we could make our own priorities, but it's not. We are called to be good and faithful stewards, which means we pursue the interests of our Master.

Before we create a budget and help our children do the same, we need to get aligned to God's purpose for the money and possessions He's entrusted to us. He wants us to grow in relationship with—and likeness to—His Son, Jesus Christ. As our spending decisions become spiritual decisions, we replace our priorities with God's in the area of money and possessions.

THREE BIGGEST TAKEAWAYS FROM THIS CHAPTER

1)

2)

3)

CHAPTER 10

Surrender

> *"In the same way, those of you who do not give up everything you have cannot be my disciples."*
>
> LUKE 14:33

Recognizing God's ownership of all things is an essential first step to learning, applying, and multiplying biblical financial principles. But it is only the first step.

The next step, surrendering your finances over to God, is equally essential. Whereas ownership was mostly a mental recognition (hard to swallow as it may have been), *surrender* requires us to take action. Just as knowing your house is on fire but choosing not to leave won't save your life, knowing God owns it all but not responding in surrender won't strengthen your relationship with Him. It will weaken it.

Jesus, in our anchor verse, calls us to surrender everything. To be clear, the surrender He calls us to does not always mean giving it all away. It means putting it back at His disposal for His use for His purposes. It is taking the next step in our development and saying, "Not only do I know it is all yours, I commit to using it the way *You* want it used to grow *Your* kingdom."

The primary battleground of surrendering our finances to God will be in creating a monthly budget that aligns our plan for earning and spending to the priorities of God from Chapter 9.

You could create a budget on a shorter or longer interval (weekly, quarterly, etc.) but monthly tends to be the simplest and most effective interval for most of us. Since most bills are paid monthly, and most income is either weekly, biweekly, twice a month, or monthly, the monthly budget cadence tends to be the best common denominator.

If you have never had a written budget before, it can sound intimidating, but it doesn't have to be complex or sophisticated. We will see the ultimate truth in this when we help our children make theirs.

If you are an old pro who has been budgeting for years, do your best to temporarily forget what you already know; try walking through the process as I describe it. In the end, you should choose whichever method of planning and tracking works for you, but first we want to do a hard reset on "the way we've always done it." This is partly to help us not get fooled into thinking we've surrendered it all when we haven't. When it is all said and done, the best budget will be the one you actually use, but I believe starting from scratch on what goes into the budget will be the best next step for most of us.

My goal in this chapter is not to make you an expert in the area of budgeting or to perfect what you already have. It is to show you a solid foundation to help you provide Modeling, Verbal Instruction, and Practical Opportunities for your children. If you want or need more guidance on your own budget, Compass offers several resources and webinars to help you reach "world-class budgeter" status! You can access them at https://compass1.org/budgeting.

BASICS OF A BUDGET

In their most basic form, every budget has two main sections, Income and Expenses. As discussed in Chapter 4, Income is all the money that comes in, and Expenses are all the money that goes out. Here's an illustration that may help. Additional tools and formats can be downloaded at the website listed above.

Income		Expenses	

Whether you use notebook paper, a spreadsheet, or a fancy online or mobile app, they all boil down to income and expenses. What comes in and what goes out.

Through this chapter, we will focus first on your budget, including both income and expenses. Once your budget is established, we will shift the discussion to how to help your kids create their own, including both income and expenses. We will walk through it one step at a time and do it all with our eyes on the eternal prize of a stronger relationship with our Lord.

CREATING YOUR BUDGET

Income
On the Income side of your budget, write down each source of income and the monthly amount you receive from that source. Some common examples of income include:

- Your job
- Your spouse's job
- Social Security

- Investment income (liquidated assets or distributions, not accrued growth or unrealized gains)
- Child support
- Government assistance (including Disability, VA, SNAP and other cash-equivalent aid)
- Cash gifts

At the bottom, create a "Total" line so you can easily see what your total income is (or is expected to be) for the month. It should look like this:

Income		Expenses	
Brian's Pay	$3,000		
Erica's Pay	$3,000		
Brian's Tie-Dye Shop	$256		
Erica's Birthday gifts	$300		
Total	$6,556		

If any of your income is variable, meaning inconsistent or not known from one month to the next, I will offer a couple of suggestions. The first is to estimate what you will receive in the month to come. While we want to honor God with every penny and dollar, insisting on exact precision is often—with regard to our faith—more an act of legalism than devotion, and with regard to time, not worth the investment.

In most cases, if you can get close, it will be close enough. For example, if you are paid hourly and you usually work between 35 and 45 hours each week, calling it 40 will probably do the trick. As an extra measure of accountability, check at the end of every month to make sure you are truly getting close (sometimes a little over and sometimes a little under). This helps ensure that you don't consistently over- or underestimate.

The second option is to use last month's income for this month's budget (what you were *actually* paid in January is what you list as your income for February). For example, if last month you earned $2,345, you can use that as this month's income on your budget; then use this month's earnings on next month's budget, and so on. If you are confused right now, you understand the primary limitation of this method. It is perfectly precise and relatively manageable but can get confusing. This method is probably best if throwing a dart is as accurate as your best income estimate. For example, if you regularly work between 3 and 55 hours each week or you just started a business and haven't built a consistent customer base, this is the better option.

Another benefit to this method is that the money is always "in the bank," so to speak. Because you are spending what you earned the previous month, rather than what you will earn this month, it resolves a lot of timing issues that can come up with a bunch of bills being due at the same time of the month, possibly before you get paid. This particular issue is also resolved by having at least a full month's expenses in your Emergency Fund, but that's a topic we'll cover in greater detail in the Expenses portion of this chapter.

For new budgeters, I would recommend using Net Pay (take-home or after-taxes pay) for the Income. Using Gross Pay gives you greater visibility to where your money is going and could inform better decisions, but those are usually more advanced measures for fine-tuning the budget rather than building a strong foundation. For example, you could modify your withholdings or change your insurance coverage to increase your take-home pay, but you shouldn't until you have prayed and developed a godly plan for your spending. Putting the cart before the horse just gives you more money to lose track of, usually never to be seen again.

We will talk more about it when we create your children's budget, but I recommend including gifts as income for a couple reasons. First, it recognizes that the gift, though given to you by a friend or family member, was truly given by God and still belongs to Him—just like everything else He's entrusted to you. It may seem like nitpicking, but fully surrendering *everything* back to God is a call to total surrender, and the slope of exceptions is a slippery one. It starts with birthday presents and soon escalates to bonuses and inheritances. Pretty soon, you could discover you are "hiding" a significant portion of God's gifts from Him.

It also sets a good precedent for your kids, since the financial gifts they receive will be a much bigger portion of their total income. They may only get $200 per year in allowance but receive

$50 for their birthday. As adults, these gifts are a cherry on top of the rest of our income, but for a kid, it is the entire dessert! We don't want them to get in the habit of excluding any portion, let alone a significant portion, of God's gifts. If you and your spouse feel strongly that money received as gifts should belong to the person they were given to—the person who received the gift should be the one to use the gift—it will be easy to do so through our Expenses. Either way, I recommend listing them as Income.

Expenses

On the expenses side of the paper, write down as many expense categories as you can think of. By expense category I mean types or groupings of things you spend money on. At this point, don't worry about the dollar amounts for each. That will be worked out in the next step. Here are some common examples and descriptions that you may want to include:

- Tithes—First fruits given to the local church
- Additional giving—Other donations or giving (not gifts)
- International Child Sponsorship—Monthly support for children in need
- Mortgage—Repayment of borrowed money for home
- Rent—Monthly payment for lease of home
- Credit card payment—Repayment of borrowed money for past months' expenses
- Car payment—Repayment of borrowed money for vehicle
- Student loan payment—Repayment of borrowed money for education
- Property taxes—Annual required taxes divided by 12 if not included in mortgage
- Homeowners' or Renters' Insurance—Insurance on home and contents if not included in mortgage
- IRA—Non-payroll savings for retirement
- College savings—Savings for future education expenses
- Natural gas—Utility payment
- Electricity—Utility payment
- Cell phone—Utility payment

- Cable/Satellite—Utility payment
- Internet—Utility payment
- Water—Utility payment
- Subscriptions—Netflix, Amazon Prime, phone apps, magazines, etc.
- Gasoline—Variable projected cost of fuel for vehicles
- HOA dues—Annual HOA dues divided by 12
- Gifts*—Total annual gift budget divided by 12
- Eating out—Non-essential dining for fun or convenience
- Clothes—Clothing needed for essential activities
- Prescriptions—Costs of predictable (non-emergency) medications
- Date night—Allocation for fun with spouse
- Lawncare—Money for fertilizer or lawnmower repairs
- Big box membership—Annual membership cost divided by 12
- Family fun—Allocation for fun as a family
- Roadside assistance—Annual cost divided by 12
- Car insurance—Annual premium divided by 12
- Car registration—Annual fees divided by 12
- Pet expenses—Food, medicine, grooming, etc.
- Necessities—Essential things you would normally buy at a grocery store
- Trash—Monthly portion of trash collection services
- Termite bond—Annual cost divided by 12
- Car repairs—Savings to repair our cars
- Your discretionary spending—Money you can spend on what you want
- Spouse's discretionary spending—Money your spouse can spend on whatever they want
- Home improvement—Money for repairing or improving your home
- Kids' activities—Sports, music, dance, etc., classes and fees
- Kids' expenses—Clothes, school supplies, sports supplies, etc. for kids
- Life insurance—Annual premium divided by 12
- Hobbies—Stuff you like to do that costs money

- Vacation—Projected cost of planned travel
- Emergency savings—Money set aside to replenish or grow financial readiness

The list is endless and unique to each of us. My expense categories may be similar to yours but will almost certainly be different because your expense categories need to match your spending habits. Like that story I told about the first time we tried to use cash and envelopes (Chapter 4), if you spend money differently than how you designed your budget, you will find it difficult to spend and track accurately.

If you find that you are spending differently (not quantitatively, but qualitatively) from the way you have structured your budget, you need to adjust. Maybe your trash and water bills are combined. No reason to separate them on the budget. If you love feeding the squirrels in winter, good for you; add an expense category or include it in another. If you generally buy your toilet paper with a cart full of groceries, combine them into a single category.

*I also recommend creating a separate gift budget to help you determine how much you will spend on gifts. This was a big miss early on for Erica and me. I came from a family where we each gave one gift to each other and gave only within the immediate family. Erica's family gave to a much larger group of people and gave much more to each person. Our first budget failed largely because I assumed she bought gifts the way I bought gifts. It took only one Christmas to realize the mismatched expectations, but we found ourselves in a hole we had to get out of because of our incorrect assumptions.

To make this gift budget, simply make a list of every gift you expect to buy during a year and about how much you will spend. For example, ours might look like this:

Brian's birthday
Erica's birthday

Weston's birthday
Barrett's Birthday
Rowan's Birthday
Eden's Birthday
Easter baskets x4
Mother's day (Leah)
Mother's day (Sue)
Mother's day (Erica)
Random weddings x2
Random graduations x3

I think you get the picture. You list them all out (birthdays, holidays, weddings, graduations, etc.) by event and person. As you work through the next step and decide how much in total you will spend on gifts, you then revisit this list and put in amounts that add up to the annual total.

Once you have all your expenses listed out, begin allocating the money you have each month (Income) into your expense categories, using God's priorities as your guide. Again, this is an essential step in truly surrendering your finances back over to God. It is great that you *know* God owns it all, but it is something entirely different to *surrender* it all to Him. Aligning our expenses to His priorities puts our faith into action.

As a reminder, God's priorities are as follows:

1. Giving
2. Providing for your family's needs
3. Meeting your financial obligations
4. Saving for the future
5. Enjoying God's abundant blessings

1) Giving. The first thing we want to do is assign dollars to our Giving expenses. As a starting point, I recommend committing to the tithe (ten percent of income). As we move further down God's priorities, we will take the opportunity to give even more, but this is where we should start.

We do not consider family gifts to be part of our Giving expense. This is because we generally see our Giving (some people refer to it as charitable giving) as financial gifts intended to advance the gospel. The gifts we give one another and our extended family members and relatives are intended to express our love for them but not really to advance the gospel. Because of this, we believe they belong at a lower priority.

This is consistent with our choice to significantly reduce our gift giving during times of financial hardship but not our Priority 1 *Tithes*. Your family should discuss whether you agree, but make sure your reasoning is based on your discernment of God's perspective on the matter, not on your own preferences.

2) Providing for essentials. Once we have assigned dollars to our Giving, we identify the *essential needs* of our family and assign dollars to cover those costs. At this point, we want to include only *essential needs*, not extra "nice-to-haves" that may be related to our *essential needs*.

For example, our family really *needs* $600 for Necessities each month, but we *prefer* to have $750. Six hundred dollars allows us to buy basic food from the grocery store—cereal, milk, bread, pasta, fruits, vegetables, etc.—but not to eat out or buy steaks, sodas, snack foods, etc. This first draft of our budget allocates $600 with more to be added later if we have surplus money as we reach lower priorities. Likewise, some gasoline is essential for getting to and from work and school, but additional gasoline may be budgeted to take a family trip. Some clothing is essential, but the new ugly Christmas sweater for your office party is just a nice-to-have.

As we move further down God's priorities for our money, we will work to create a surplus that enables us to add some of the nice-to-haves back into higher priority categories. But for now, we need to stick with the essentials.

3) Meeting financial obligations. Next we move to financial obligations—the money we owe. From our remaining income, we assign the minimum payments due. If we find we still have money remaining after paying the minimum on all financial obligations, we can pay above that to reduce our balance. Credit cards,* loans (including mortgages, car payments, etc.), taxes, and required premiums and fees belong in this priority. And as always, we look for any surplus that can be reallocated to expanding the higher Priority 1 and 2 opportunities (giving and meeting more of the needs of our families).

> *Be sure to allocate spending on a credit card to its true expense category so that it doesn't get lost in the "Credit Card" bucket. The Credit Card expense line should be dedicated to paying down the balance from *previous* months. All *new* spending should be accounted for under its more accurate expense category. This is one of the big reasons we have always reverted to cash as our primary currency (see Chapter 4). Shuffling through credit card transactions to figure out which purchases belonged in which expense categories always ended up being more trouble than it was worth, from our perspective.

4) Saving for the future. Now we look at saving, ensuring we are putting away a reasonable amount (not too much and not too little) to sustain our giving, providing, and meeting obligations in times of financial hardship.

Our first saving priority should be building an emergency fund. The minimum emergency fund I recommend is one month's worth of expenses. This number is strategic in that it allows you to stop worrying about the timing of bills coming due. As difficult as it is to create your first budget, it gets much more difficult when you have to juggle things because of the due dates of various payments. By having one full month's expenses in reserve, it won't matter whether every bill is due on the same day or whether you are able to spread them across the month. Either way, you will still have a full month's expenses in the bank at the end of the month once you have balanced your expenses and income (what went out came in, and what came in went out).

One month's expenses, however, don't cover much of an emergency these days. I recommend adding to this fund every month until you reach around six month's expenses. If you are a single-income family, you may want to land a little higher. If you and your spouse each have full-time jobs or a second income of some kind, you could probably have less. It is unlikely that all your income streams would dry up at the same time. Once again, this is something for you and your spouse to discuss and discern together. We want to keep in mind that the purpose of our savings is to allow us to continue giving, providing, and meeting our financial obligations in times of hardship, not to achieve independence from God. Set prayerfully-discerned goals and make steady progress toward them. When you reach your goal, shift future resources back to giving and paying down obligations, rather than building bigger barns (see Luke 12 – it doesn't end well.)

5) Enjoying God's blessings. Finally, we allocate funds to the "nice-to-haves" in life. Once again, as we examine our past spending, we reevaluate dedicating some surplus for higher priorities—additional giving opportunities, meeting more needs of our families, accelerating the repayment of money we owe, and more quickly meeting our savings goals.

You have probably noticed that I have left out most of my recommendations as to which expenses fall into which priorities. That is intentional. Again, my goal is to build a foundation specifically for the purposes of helping you surrender your finances back over to God, align your spending with His priorities, and train your children to do the same. I am confident that if you seek God's counsel in prayer with a heart of true and sincere surrender, He will give you the discernment necessary to bring Him glory. And your surrender will be modeled, explained, and provided well to your children.

In the end, your simple budget may look something like this (this is not my recommendation of what your budget *should* look like, only an example of what it *could* look like).

Income		Expenses	
Brian's Pay	$3,000	Tithe	$700
Erica's Pay	$3,000	Support of Compass	$100
Brian's Tie-Dye Shop	$256	Support of Bible Project	$100
Erica's Birthday gifts	$300	Support of Orphanage	$100
		Support of YouVersion	$100
Total	$6,556	Rent	$1,000
		Car Insurance	$70
		Car Registration	$50
		Gifts	$200
		Natural Gas	$125
		Cell Phone	$55
		Gasoline	$300
		Internet	$60
		Subscriptions	$75
		Medical Insurance	$500
		HOA Dues	$55
		Property Taxes	$250
		Home Insurance	$80
		Family Fun	$100
		AAA	$15
		Necessities	$750
		Brian's Discretionary	$100
		Erica's Discretionary	$400
		Kids' Allowance	$176
		Home Improvements	$100
		Haircuts	$75
		Trash Service	$50
		Kids Expenses	$100
		Life Insurance	$70
		Vacation Savings	$300
		Emergency Savings	$300
		Car Repairs	$100
		Total	$6,556

Addressing an Unbalanced Budget

If you find that you have more Income than Expenses, go back and balance your budget by adding additional amounts based on God's priorities until every dollar of Income is accounted for in your Expenses. Go in order of God's priorities, beginning with Giving and ending with Enjoying His Blessings.

If you find that you have more Expenses than Income, there are three ways to resolve this. The first, and least effective, is to increase your income. Seems crazy that someone would advise *against* increasing income, but I have learned from experience that increasing your income without an effective plan for controlling spending will have little to no impact on your bottom line. As

Luke 16:10 points out, if we are not faithful with a little, we cannot and will not be trusted with a lot.

Before our financial crisis, Erica and I significantly increased our income but had no plan for controlling our expenses. The result? We were broke when we were making $30,000 one year and we were broke when we were making $75,000 the next year. Where did the extra $45,000 go? I have no clue. I mean that. We lived in a basic house with basic cars. No addictions or luxurious vacations. No savings or investments to speak of. It was just gone. We did not pay any more attention to where the $75,000 went than we did with the $30,000.

That was the first approach. The second is to go back through your expenses and make cuts. This hurts, but it is an effective first step to balancing your budget. When Erica and I got serious about getting our finances in order, it was tough. We had no date nights, no family fun, no discretionary money, no vacations.

We had to slash our $3,000 annual gift budget down to $750. Imagine the conversations with extended family members who might think our change in gifting indicated a lack of love. Yes, awkward but necessary.

We prioritized cable, internet, and both cell phones over other luxuries. It was painful, but we had learned our lesson about increasing income without addressing our spending habits. We recommend you start there.

The final and best approach is to do both. Address your spending habits and increase your income at the same time. For many, this may seem like an unrealistic plan, but you don't need to think in extremes. You don't necessarily have to get a second job. For Erica and me, it was just the small annual increases and occasional promotions we received at work. Most years, it was only two to three percent, but it added a little more income while we controlled our spending and paid down debt.

Through this steady plodding approach, it was only a matter of months before we could add a little discretionary spending for each of us each month. Then family fun and date nights. Those aren't big ticket items, but they are big morale boosters that help drive contentment rather than consumption in our lives. After a few years we were even able to increase our gift budget.

If you try all this and are still unable to create a budget that meets all the Priority 1-3 expenses in your life, please reach out to Compass through our website for additional assistance. We can connect you with a budgeting coach to help you work through more extreme strategies for balancing your budget.

Monthly Review

This budget should be revisited each month and adjusted for inevitable fluctuations. Natural gas bills go up in the winter and back down in the summer. Out-of-town trips will require more gasoline this month than last. Back-to-school shopping probably doesn't need to show up every month, but you will want to build it into your budget each August.

The question we ask every month is, "Do we have anything special going on this month?" Many line items will be the same from one month to the next, but you should reevaluate them on a regular basis to make sure your plan—and your expectations—represent your current reality.

CREATING YOUR CHILDREN'S BUDGET

Once we have aligned our use of money to God's priorities, we are in the right position to train our children to do the same. To reinforce what we have already discussed, we should provide Modeling to our kids by involving them in our budgeting efforts; Verbal Instruction about how and why we have chosen to allocate money to certain expense categories and not to others; and now Practical Opportunities for them to follow us as we follow Christ.

Our children's budget will look a lot like ours: Income on one side, Expenses on the other. They will have fewer sources of income and fewer expenses, but the same format will work well. For our kids, though, we prefer a weekly budget rather than the monthly budget we have for our whole family. Since they don't have monthly bills, that specific advantage we discussed for our budgets doesn't apply.

We also distribute allowance weekly because we find smaller

quantities of money help reinforce a steady plodding mentality as they see small amounts adding up over time. The alternative dumps a relatively large amount of money in their lap once a month, leading to dollar-sign eyes like Scrooge McDuck. With a weekly budget, we are also able to reinforce godly budgeting principles with greater repetition because it provides them 52 Practical Opportunities each year rather than 12.

We begin budgeting with our kids when they turn six. Before that, they were not really getting anything out of it. They didn't understand what they were saving for and really were just happy to have money.

We generally follow the same income and expense strategy for the younger kids—but without the formal planning and tracking of a written budget. Overall, we have seen the younger kids without a budget learning as much about godly financial principles as when we had the first few kids do a budget at an earlier age. If you think your younger children will benefit from having a budget, give it a shot. The earlier they start, the more likely it is to become their baseline for life.

Income[12]

As we have previously established, every budget is made up of two key parts: income and expenses. This leads to one of the most profound yet obvious ideas you will learn in this book: in order for children to learn to honor God with their finances, they need to *have* finances (income and expenses). This, of course, presents an equally obvious problem: kids don't naturally have incomes or expenses. Because going to school is their work, they have no income. And instead of expenses, they eat all *our* food.

Let me rephrase that: we provide for and financially support them while they are in school, so they have no expenses. Like the Spirit jumpstarting our dead souls, if we are going to provide our kids Practical Opportunities to apply biblical financial principles, we have to supplement the natural cycle.

Enter the allowance.

There are two views of how to provide your kids with an allowance. The first is that you assign them household chores and pay them for their work. This is great because it not only provides them with income but also teaches them how adult employment works (you get paid for the work you do but get paid nothing if you don't work).

The second view is that children should be expected to help with household chores—not to earn income—but because it is the socially responsible thing to do. As members of the household, they should help maintain the house. As those who will eat the food, they should help prepare and/or clean up.

Both views are very defensible, and it is another one of those things you and your spouse need to prayerfully discern for your own family. I won't judge you either way, and neither should anyone else. As long as your reasoning is based on your discernment of God's perspective, not your own or anyone else's, God will honor your decision.

Our family has landed on the second method. We give an allowance regardless of the chores they do, but we expect them to do chores. We mainly landed on this because some of our children were not motivated by money in their early years (and that's not necessarily a bad thing). We would ask them to do their chores so they could earn money, and they would politely respond, "No thanks." We would explain that if they didn't do their chores, they wouldn't receive their allowance. They would politely say, "Okay. I understand."

Again, they have no real expenses, so there was very little urgency—especially at a young age. The natural consequences were not immediate enough to get their attention. This blew up the whole idea of them having finances to dedicate to God; we were back to no income and no expenses. As they have gotten older and have more expensive "wants," we could probably transition to a pay-for-chores approach, but we probably won't. Giving them an allowance and expecting them to do chores independent of that allowance has been effective, so we will likely stick with it. Until it's not.

Our system is that each child gets one dollar each week for each year of age, starting at three years old. The four-year-old gets $4 each week. The seven-year-old gets $7 each week. The ten-year-old gets $10 each week. Our thirteen-year-old gets $13 each week. But he also gets an additional $10 per week as pay for cleaning the bathrooms, the offer we made to help him get a cell phone.

If you do the math on these, they may seem like a lot, but we are giving them income specifically for the purpose of giving them expenses. As you will soon see, this amount of money ends up being extremely limiting and will require them to make some real decisions on what they want most, what they will do without, and how to achieve balance.

From time to time, they will help a neighbor and get a few extra dollars. Or maybe an old lady at the grocery store thinks they are cute enough that they should get a dollar. All this goes in as income, too, along with any cash gifts they receive throughout the year.

As kids get older and start a part-time job, any income they earn will be added to their budget just as it is with ours.

Expenses

Since we have successfully given our children income, we can now work on getting them expenses. As we did with our own budgets, we will work through God's priorities in sequence.

1) Giving. Each of our kids is required to give at least ten percent to the church we attend. We talk them through the reasons why God wants us to give, explaining that we give too. As other opportunities for giving come up, we encourage them to give above and beyond the tithe, but we don't require it.

2) Providing for essentials. Most children will not have any expenses related to providing for their families. Some parents with older kids may want them to contribute to basic food and housing needs. My only guidance on this is to make sure you have explained it well and approach it in a productive and Bible-based manner, such as, "Becoming an adult comes with a lot of responsibilities. I know this seems harsh and unreasonable, but it's preparing you to be a more responsible adult, and that's a goal we have for you."

They may not see the logic in it at the time, but it will make more sense to them later when they experience the benefits of the decision.

3) Meeting financial obligations. Younger children will also have very few financial obligations, especially debt. The exception, as previously discussed, is our thirteen-year-old who has a cell phone, and therefore a cell phone bill. Each month, he has to pay that bill through us. If at any point he is unable to pay, the phone gets shut off.

Another one of our children wanted to upgrade an online educational game to the Premium package. He is responsible for saving up throughout the year and choosing whether to renew that subscription. Adding expectations like paying for their own gasoline and insurance is another great way to expose older kids to the financial obligations adults have.

4) Saving for the future. We require our children to save ten percent of their income. This will be used for college expenses or after. Again, this simple and basic expectation builds the baseline experience that saving, like giving, is an essential part of our financial lives. We share the reasons for—and advantages to—saving for the future, but even if they don't understand them now, they are building the habit of saving.

Another way we incorporate saving—and the vast majority of their expense categories—is by requiring them to buy each other's birthday and Christmas gifts. They set the total amount they want to save for each gift and then work toward getting that amount saved by the time it is needed. Each child has a birthday and Christmas gift envelope for each sibling and parent, in addition to Mothers' Day and Fathers' Day. We help them prioritize based on what will be needed first and coach them as they go, but for the most part, we allow them to make their own decisions.

5) Enjoying God's blessings. After they've met the higher priorities, they usually have a few dollars left for things that are fun. The four-year-old just thinks it's fun to have money, and she rarely spends any except for fast food. The seven-year-old wants packs of Pokémon cards and Wendy's. The ten-year-old wants donuts, McDonald's, and Pokémon cards. The thirteen-year-old just wants the newest iPhone (and a Tesla). Once we get to this point, we pretty much let them use the money as they choose. We'll discuss the few exceptions in the next chapter.

Another fun discovery we've made has been the gift of restaurant gift cards. One year, my mom got the kids gift cards to their favorite fast-food restaurant and to Dairy Queen (her favorite fast-food restaurant). As you would expect, they immediately asked if they could go and spend theirs. We just went with it. They asked again the next day and we said we would take them but warned them that it would use up the rest of the money on the card and they would be out. At that moment, the light bulbs went on for them. And for *us*. We had stumbled on the currency they respected more than cash!

The gift cards somehow represented freedom and spending power more than actual currency. They better understood the power of their decisions, the limited nature of money, and how to delay gratification. It was amazing! We've embraced it and regularly encourage friends and family to get them restaurant gift cards for most birthdays and holidays.

We still go out to eat as a family on the family's budget from time to time, but if they want something special on any given day, they know they will be responsible for buying it. We are faithful to take them when they ask, with the rare exception of a logistical issue with taking them. I think they have learned more about responsible spending through this exercise than any other.

Weekly Review
Your children's budgets should be revisited each week. Some lines will stay the same, but as one gift's savings is filled, another will be started. Out-of-town trips are a good time for children to save a little money so they can buy a drink at a gas station (not sure why that is so fun for kids, but it is). Or you can encourage them to save up for souvenirs on an upcoming vacation. Again, they do not usually have the long-term vision to save for next summer's vacation through the whole year, but they will absolutely take the

bait six or eight weeks out as they dream of the random things they will buy at the quirky store they remember from last time.

CLOSING THOUGHTS

We got awfully tactical this chapter, but I don't want us to lose sight of the goal. A budget is a plan, and plans can be good. Like the law of the Old Testament, however, a plan alone will not bring glory to God (Romans 3:20). It must be a plan grounded in faithfulness. It must be a plan anchored in God's ownership. And it must be a plan that leads us to true surrender.

It's God's money. It's His stuff. He has entrusted it to us, but with a purpose—to develop and refine us so that we can be made more into the likeness of Jesus with every decision we make.

We should have the same goal with our children. We do not give them income just so they can give it, spend it, or save it. We give them income so they can learn to glorify God throughout their lives with the godly use of His money, so that they can be made more into the likeness of Jesus with every decision they make.

THREE BIGGEST TAKEAWAYS FROM THIS CHAPTER

1)

2)

3)

CHAPTER 11

Choice

*"No one can serve two masters. Either you will
hate the one and love the other, or you will be
devoted to the one and despise the other. You
cannot serve God and money."*

MATTHEW 6:24

At some point in our lives, most of us have felt the conviction of the Spirit to begin doing something that brings Him glory or to stop doing something that diminishes His glory. We go about our daily lives for years, or even decades, unaware of a particular sin until the day God reveals it to us and we immediately feel the incredible burden to confess and repent. The sin we had overlooked in our lives for so long becomes as obvious as a purple school bus parked in our front yard and can no longer be ignored.

Repentance, though, means more than just acknowledging that something is wrong. It requires us to turn away from that sin—to, in Jesus' own words, *"Go now and leave your life of sin"* (John 8:11).

Too often, that conviction to live more consistently with God's desires fades. Like a New Year's resolution abandoned by January 15, we begin to diminish the impact of our failure and forget the burning of that burden. Now that we have recognized God's ownership of all things and surrendered our finances back to

Him through a budget aligned to His priorities, we must continue pushing forward by executing our plan for His glory.

The Pillar of Choice (introduced in Chapter 8) centers around the teaching from our anchor verse, Matthew 6:24. As we said previously, this verse comes out of Jesus' Sermon on the Mount. Jesus could have chosen from any number of idols to address, but He chose money. As we know, Jesus was an amazing speaker and teacher. His parables were layered with meaning and continue to reveal "new" truths each time we read them. His sermons and speeches spoke to unique groups within a single audience and delivered unique convictions and encouragements—all with the same set of words.

Given His divine level of articulation, we can't believe He simply picked the topic of money out of a hat for this teaching. He wasn't sitting around that morning thinking about five or six things He could use to complete the sentence, *"You cannot serve God and . . ."* and just happened to pick money. He chose money because it is the chief competition for the commitment, worship, and glory in our lives that should belong to Him.

Many Bible translations replace "money" with "Mammon" in this particular verse, which conveys the spirit we often assign to money. By "spirit," I mean the invisible, energizing, and animating force by which money distracts and corrupts us. Whether we believe money has its own spirit (Mammon) or is simply an inanimate stumbling block placed in our paths, we must recognize that Jesus saw it as a serious competitor, a thief of God's rightful glory. We must not underestimate its ability to impact the choices we make.

This chapter assumes three things: first, that the Spirit has convicted you about your relationship with money; second, that you genuinely want to execute a plan that is aligned to God's priorities; and third, that you want to help your children do the same.

To help you succeed, I will point out some common issues that come up as we try to live by the budgets we have made. I'll also share some best practices we have found over the years. Then, I will again turn the conversation to how you can incorporate these best practices into your children's financial plans.

CHOOSING GOD OVER MONEY

Currency

As discussed in previous chapters, our choice of currency can have a significant impact on our ability to execute our plan. Nowhere in Scripture will you find God taking a position on whether you should pay with paper or plastic, but it is clear that once we have committed a plan to God, we should follow through (Luke 9:62, James 4:17), modifying it only when we: (a) believe God is pointing us in another direction, (b) have new information, or (c) have a better understanding of old information, which merits a change.

If you conclude that recording and tracking your expenses in their appropriate expense categories is impractical, inconvenient, or downright impossible, it is very likely that you will abandon your efforts to follow your budget. Don't despair! You can find a variety of tools to help you track expenses at https://compass1.org/tools-for-your-journey/. Still, each will require discipline and a plan—even for how you will hold yourself accountable to hold yourself accountable.

Do you and your spouse commit to saving all receipts and reconciling them every night before you forget what they were for? Do you plan to scrub credit card and bank account statements at the end of each month? Whatever the plan is, you need to work through it and commit to revisiting and revising it regularly.

Your first plan will not be perfect. You should accept that now. Neither will your ninety-ninth. But, like learning to ride a bike, there is a big difference between falling off and getting back up and falling off and giving up. This is why Erica and I choose cash for most of our expenses. Having fallen off the bike enough times and finding we didn't have the discipline to track our spending other ways, we reverted to cash in envelopes, with a few exceptions.

These exceptions all meet two basic criteria: first, that we have discipline to not overspend in the excepted area; second, that we will be able to identify these expenses quickly and easily so that we can be sure we stayed true to our plan. If either of these is not true for an expense category, we use cash. Here's more about how the exceptions show up in our lives.

Exception: low-risk expense categories. The first exception to our cash-only plan is the categories we see as low risk, meaning there is very little risk that we will lose track or cheat. For example, we don't pay our utilities with cash. The heat is on 68 in the winter and the AC is on 72 in the summer. We don't find ourselves tempted to change that very much based on our finances. When the bill comes, whether it is higher or lower than expected, we are going to pay what we owe.

Gasoline is another low-risk category. We don't get any particular joy or satisfaction from filling up the tank, so we are not tempted to splurge on gas when we have an exceptionally good or bad day. We get gas only when we need it, and that is a fairly predictable need. Furthermore, with four kids, the last thing I want to do is go into a gas station. It is frowned upon (if not illegal) to leave some of them in the car. But if I take them in, they have an urge to buy stuff.

Since the only thing we buy at a gas station is fuel, identifying those transactions on a credit card or bank statement is pretty cut and dried.

In either of these examples, if we find we are consistently spending more than we planned, we make adjustments on future budgets.

Exception: "electronic envelopes". The next exception we have learned to make is the use of what we call "electronic envelopes." The advantage of an envelope with cash is that it is easy to see what money is there; you no longer need to track individual transactions. If you put $100 into an envelope at the beginning of the month and you have $20 in there now, you spent $80. You may want to pull receipts and see exactly what you bought, but you will not be able to accidentally overspend if the cash is gone.

In the beginning of our budgeting efforts, we stuffed an envelope with cash for our gift budget—and ran into a complicated issue. Nearly all the gifts I bought were bought online. I would buy something on Amazon, paying with a debit or credit card, and have to figure out how to make change with other envelopes. It was a nightmare. Looking for a better solution, we came up with a separate bank account and debit card specifically for gifts. We set up an automatic direct deposit so that a set amount from every paycheck goes into that account, which we use only for gifts. Since only gift money goes in and only gift money goes out, staying accountable is easy.

Likewise, we have a specific credit card we use for all "Necessities." Since all Necessities are purchased using that card and nothing but Necessities are purchased on that card, Erica and I are able to easily track how much has been spent and how much we have left.

Exception: major purchases. The final exception we make is that of major purchases. When we have a large one-time expense that has already been discussed and agreed upon, we will often pay with a credit or debit card (not the debit card for Gifts or the Necessities card) as opposed to carrying around a lot of cash.

For example, our refrigerator door is getting ready to fall off its hinges and the light flickers like a strobe, so we have set aside money to buy a new one. It is built into our budget and the money is available when we find the one we want for the price we want. Likewise, our minivan was making some crazy noises last month and we knew it would need major repairs soon. Because of the size of these types of things, it will be hard to miss or mistake them on the statements. Nor is there much risk that we will lose our discipline and just decide to throw in a new set of chrome rims for the van or overspend on the replacement refrigerator. Because we are confident that we will stay within our budget and can easily isolate these expenses from the others, we would rather not withdraw thousands of dollars and have it laying around the house.

Again, let's remember our purpose. It is not to prescribe a certain method—i.e. cash vs card—but to accomplish a certain goal—accountable vs not. God doesn't take a position on cash, card, or e-currency. The goal is discipline, execution, and accountability to our God-aligned plan, not the exclusive or preferred use of any particular form of money. I have personally found it easier and more effective to do that using cash, but if you can do it using credit or debit cards, use them. Model their use, explain it to your kids, and guide them in doing the same. If you have a system that uses Venmo or other e-currency, awesome! Model it, explain it, and help your kids glorify God with e-money. Accountability is the goal, not currency.

Establishing Negotiables and Non-Negotiables

As you already know, once you have been convicted by the Spirit, have confessed your failures, and committed yourself to following God in a particular area of your life, Satan takes notice and begins his attack. As long as you stay passive and non-committal in your obedience to God, he doesn't bother you much. But when you take a stand and begin doing something bold in a new and big way, he responds in force, and we should be prepared to resist his efforts (Ephesians 6:10-13). But God always offers us a way to resist (James 4:6-8). One of the best ways to defend against his attacks is to establish negotiables and non-negotiables for your finances in advance by spending time in God's word and prayerful discernment of His truths.

Our family has agreed that we can move money from one expense category to another as needed (negotiable), but the money has to come from somewhere (non-negotiable) and can come only from an expense category of equal or lower priority (non-negotiable). For example, if it is close to the end of the month and we need to buy milk and bananas (Priority 2), we can move money from Family Fun or Discretionary (both Priority 5), but not out of Giving (Priority 1). These types of things happen almost every month (more on adapting a budget mid-month a little later in this chapter), so having ground rules established based on our convictions rather than our emotions helps us choose God over money when temptation arises.

Another non-negotiable for us is debt. We have used debt in the past and agree we will not again, regardless of circumstances. We know that things will come up that make us want to go back into debt, so deciding before those things come up helps give us strength and perseverance.

Part of me wants to avoid going any deeper on the topic of debt because, in many ways, it has become the focus of too many Christian financial methodologies. Just because a person is debt-free does not mean they are glorifying God with their finances; and a person can bring glory to God while still in debt.

The Christian financial world has falsely depicted debt as the battleground of faithfulness and freedom. But make no mistake, *the heart*, not *the wallet*, is the battleground of faithfulness and freedom. The presence or absence of debt is only an outward expression of what's in our hearts.

So while I began this discourse saying part of me didn't want to go into it, the greater part of me, as you can probably tell, wants to share my perspective with the hope of helping people make the right decisions for the right reasons. With that in mind, let's just tackle the topic head-on.

Is debt a sin? No. From a legalistic perspective, "Do not borrow money from anyone" is not a direct command or instruction in Scripture. Debt, however, is always depicted as a bad thing in Scripture, and financial freedom is always a good thing (Deuteronomy 15:6, Proverbs 22:7, Matthew 5:42). Likewise, we are told that when we find ourselves in debt we should repay as quickly as possible (Psalm 37:21, Proverbs 3:27-28, Romans 13:8). So even if it is not a sin, we should avoid it and handle it, at the very least, with extreme care.

However, like the expert in the law who asked Jesus who his neighbor was (Luke 10:29), I believe, "Is debt a sin?" is the wrong question to ask. Hopefully we are asking the question with the motives of honoring God with our decisions rather than trying to justify ourselves, as the expert in the law was doing, but even so, it is still looking for an oversimplified answer and a check-the-box solution. The right question, I believe, is, "Are my motives for taking on debt God-glorifying and consistent with the fruit of the Spirit?" Erica and I have decided that, for us, they are not.

When I meditate on the reasons I want to take on debt, I find there are three primary motivations.

First, I want *more* than what God has provided for me. For example, as our family prepares to relocate this upcoming summer, we find that God has provided enough money for a three-bedroom, two-bathroom house on ten acres *or* a four-bedroom, three-bathroom house on one acre. With four kids and out-of-town relatives and the random desire to own a sheep, I, of course, would like a four-bedroom, three-bathroom house on ten acres (the best of both). God hasn't provided that for me, though, so using debt to cover the difference would be an expression of discontentment.

Second, I want *now* what God has not provided for me *yet*. While God has not provided enough for that four-bedroom, three-bathroom house on ten acres yet, He has given me marketable skills and a good and stable job so I should be able to afford it later. I want to take advantage of His provision and buy *now* what I expect to be able to afford *later*. For me, using debt this way would be an expression of impatience.

Finally, I know God hasn't provided this for me yet and that I should be content with what He has provided, but I want to buy it anyway. "These perfect houses just keep popping up and selling and we are missing out. I know I'm being discontented and impatient, but I have passed up the last ten, so I will just do it anyway. I know I will probably regret it, but we have to do something or we are going to end up living in someone's garage next summer!" When all else fails, Satan appeals to my lack of self-control and tries to push me against what I know is good and right.

For us, debt, although not quite a sin in and of itself, is an expression of underlying sinful desires. Jesus, who was never discontented, impatient, or lacking self-control, never saw the need to go into debt. I will certainly never be as holy as Jesus, but I intend to die trying.

Avoiding debt for reasons like these are small victories we can win for God's glory. Maybe you can relate to these reasons and maybe you can't, but I challenge you to truly investigate your motives for taking on, or staying in, debt. For us, it is a non-negotiable. Because we have already prayerfully wrestled with and concluded the matter, we are able to stand with more confidence against the temptations of the enemy. While you may decide differently than we have, do so *before* you have the urge to buy something using debt, and do it only because it is consistent with the Spirit and the will of God, not because it is easy, convenient, or socially acceptable.

Accountability Partners

The next way we can consistently choose God over money in our day-to-day lives is by developing a strong network of accountability partners. Proverbs 15:22 teaches us, *"Plans fail for lack of counsel, but with many advisors they succeed."* Ecclesiastes 4:12 says, *"Though one may be overpowered, two can defend themselves. A cord of three strands is not quickly broken."* Proverbs 27:17 establishes that, *"As iron sharpens iron, so one person sharpens another."* One of the greatest gifts God has given us to help us stay faithful to Him is the community of believers around us. In choosing counsel and accountability partners, we want to make sure they share our values, understand our goals, and are willing to speak the truth to us in love.

Similar to our conversation in Chapter 3 of establishing a common vision with our spouse, advisors who do not share or understand our goals may offer counsel that is well-meaning and perhaps even wise but does not fulfill the purpose we intend.

In 2 Corinthians 6:14, Paul instructs the church to *"not be yoked together with unbelievers."* This has nothing to do with farming and is not a call for the Church to isolate itself from the rest of the world; neither Jesus nor Paul did that. Rather, it is a call to recognize that unbelievers have fundamentally different goals and objectives than followers of Christ. We need to put up reasonable boundaries to ensure we do not enter into relationships where our different goals could lead to confusion or the compromising of our convictions. By seeking counsel from strong believers, we expect to receive Bible-based and Spirit-filled perspectives that align to our goals, enrich our own perspective, and test our convictions.

We should regularly seek these accountability partners when we need to make significant decisions, including major purchases or changes in priorities, both long- and short-term. The first of these accountability partners should always be our spouse, but we should also look for others who can remain objective when our spouse's perspectives may be too similar to ours.

About a year after Erica and I had decided to seriously attack paying off our mortgage, we realized it would be extremely helpful to fence in our back yard. Our neighborhood is pretty safe and cars generally drive at reasonable speeds, but with four kids, a couple dogs, and a bunch of chickens, a fence would really make life easier. Erica and I discussed it, counted the cost, and wanted to move forward with the fence. Next, I called a trustworthy accountability partner and explained the idea to him. He tested me with questions like:

- Are you confident that your estimate will be the full cost or will other expenses show up later?
- How long will you be delaying paying off your mortgage if you get the fence now?
- Are there lower-cost alternatives that get the job done?
- What would be the downside of just toughing it out until you pay off the mortgage?
- What's your real goal with this change and trade-off?

At the end of the conversation, he agreed that getting the fence provided enough short-term benefit to delay paying off the mortgage an extra two months, but I left the conversation more confident about the decision.

That same accountability partner called me a few months later to ask for my perspective on a major purchase he and his wife were considering. We had a very similar conversation, only in reverse. Proverbs 27:17 in action!

In the end, you and your spouse—not the accountability partners—make the decision, but their counsel will add insight and confidence to your own understanding and discernment.

Benchmarks and Goals

The next tool for consistently choosing God over money is to establish a series of smaller goals and contingency plans as you work toward your larger goals. This exercise allows us to think ahead about how we want to handle both the small victories and the defeats we will encounter so we don't lose sight of our long-term goals or the motivation to achieve them.

When I help others build their budgets, I take them through an exercise I call, "When we . . . we will . . . ." In this exercise, you simply make a list of possible and likely events, good and bad, and decide how you will respond. Here are some examples:

- When we have an unexpected and unbudgeted expense over $100, we will discuss together what to do.
- When we pay off our first student loan, we will go out to a nice dinner to celebrate.
- When we want to buy something over $500 (non-emergency), we will talk to an accountability partner and wait at least one month.
- When we pay off our first student loan, we will take half the monthly payment and increase our giving while the other half gets snowballed into the next student loan.
- When we pay off each car loan, we will save half of the monthly payment for the purchase of our next car and donate the other half to ministries advancing the gospel.
- When we get our tax refund, we will use half of it to pay down debt and half for a small family vacation.
- When we get pay increases at work, we will give 50 percent of the increase to ministries advancing the gospel.

These are not meant to be binding contracts or a new set of boxes to check. They are intended to help us come up with intentional plans when we have a clear vision of our goals—*before* the emergency or blessing hits and our emotions distract us. These plans can and should be reviewed periodically. We can always modify our plans if God leads us that way, but starting with a prayerfully discerned plan for the expected and unexpected will help us make progress toward the long-term goals we have.

Adjusting Mid-Month

This ties in with several of the other best practices we have covered, but I think it deserves its own section. Let me ruin the surprise for you: your plan is going to fail. Probably the very first month. I know it doesn't make you feel warm and fuzzy, but it is the truth. The only thing more demotivating than being told the road is going to be long and bumpy is finding out for yourself.

Erica and I have been budgeting for 13 years now, and most months still have to be adjusted mid-month. Life happens. But with a plan aligned to God's priorities, the conviction and support of the Holy Spirit, and the accountability of trusted partners, we can push through.

When it happens, go back to the basics. Look at how the new expense impacts the rest of your plan. Find lower-priority items you can pull from. If that doesn't cover it, use your Emergency Savings but plan to replenish it the following month(s) to get back to your target.

Three days after writing this chapter, a great example of a mid-month adjustment came up. It's a few weeks before Christmas, and Erica is trying to get everything ready. She's baking treats for the kids' teachers, getting together with friends one last time before the holidays start, and getting the house ready for guests. A couple of our kids woke up at five o'clock this morning (needing Mom's attention) and today is the last day of school before Christmas Break (not a break for her). When Erica got home from running errands around lunch, it was clear that the day had defeated her. She needed a break, so I offered to take care of dinner.

The problem is, we didn't budget for this. We have a monthly fund called "LMNOD" (Loving Mother's Night-Off Dinner) to give Erica a night-off dinner each month, but I had plans to use that the week between Christmas and New Year. The non-negotiables in this situation are that she's getting tacos and the money has to come from a lower priority. Where the money comes from is negotiable, though. Shuffling through our envelopes, I find that our options are:

Option 1: Use LMNOD and scrap the plans for later in the month. I know she's going to be stressed when all the guests leave, and she's going to need another night-off dinner, so although it is an option, it isn't an ideal option.

Option 2: Lump it in with Necessities. Our Necessities budget is mostly Priority 2 but has some Priority 5 as well. Eating out doesn't usually fall into our Necessities spending, but we can choose to spend it that way this time and reduce the amount we have for true necessities for the month. I don't like this option because Erica is generally in charge of this line item of the budget; using it now will cause her stress later when she tries to finish the month within budget.

Option 3: I can use my own Discretionary money. I have $80 left, which will cover the cost of the tacos and leave me about $30 for the rest of the month.

Option 4: I can use Erica's Discretionary money. This is a terrible option. Making her pay for her own night off, which I suggested, isn't consistent with my goal of showing her how much I love her.

Option 5: Family Fun has $134 in it and we don't really have any clear plan for this money. We have some other Christmas-related categories that will cover the cost of some of the things we had planned, so this money is very much available.

Option 6: I can consider this to be an Emergency and overspend for the month, making sure I replenish our Emergency Fund next month.

In the end, I decided to use the Family Fun money. After the $50 for dinner, we still have $84, which will cover a couple ice cream runs and a few other activities for Christmas Break. I made this decision unilaterally because talking it out with Erica would only stress her out more. But because of our family's preestablished non-negotiables, and since we've had lots of these types of conversations before, I'm confident the decision is in line with our agreed goals and objectives.

These types of things happen often. It's important that we learn to manage these exceptions without abandoning our plan to honor God by aligning our priorities to His.

There will be times when the whole thing falls off the rails and we find ourselves way off track, but we can't just give up. In one of my manufacturing roles, we had our own internal saying,

"Let's make it a good, bad day." What it meant was, even if the day started terribly, the machines didn't run right, a bunch of employees called in sick, and the other shift left us a mess, we had the choice to let the rest of the day be a mess too, or to do the best we could to salvage it and have a good, bad day.

These bad days are, in fact, where our faithfulness is tested and proven. In Psalm 15, David wrote:

> ¹Lord, who may dwell in your sacred tent?
> Who may live on your holy mountain?
>
> ²The one whose walk is blameless,
> who does what is righteous,
> who speaks the truth from their heart;
>
> ³whose tongue utters no slander,
> who does no wrong to a neighbor,
> and casts no slur on others;
>
> ⁴who despises a vile person
> but honors those who fear the Lord;
> who keeps an oath even when it hurts,
> and does not change their mind;
>
> ⁵who lends money to the poor without interest;
> who does not accept a bribe against the innocent.
> Whoever does these things
> will never be shaken.

While we would no doubt prefer to avoid these challenges and tests, working through them while remaining faithful to our commitment to choose God over money allows us to say with confidence that we, too, will never be shaken. When things are easy, we become complacent and weak, but when we have to struggle and persevere, we are strengthened in both our ability and our resolve.

Too often, new budgeters have one issue come up, get discouraged because their plan didn't work, and scrap the rest of the month, making their financial positions even worse than they started (usually with the promise of starting anew the following month). Don't give in to this kind of thinking. Habakkuk 3:17-18 says, *"Though the fig tree does not bud and there are no grapes on the vines, though the olive crop fails and the fields produce no food, though there are no sheep in the pen and no cattle in the stalls, yet I will rejoice in the LORD, I will be joyful in God my Savior."*

My version would go something like this, "Though the van needs a new flywheel and the refrigerator door is falling off, though my budget is way off and Christmas is three weeks away, though I do not know why this is happening or how to plan for next month, still I will dedicate my finances to God and live by His priorities and principles the best I can, trusting Him to provide."

TEACHING OUR CHILDREN TO CHOOSE GOD OVER MONEY

Currency

For younger children, cash will be the obvious currency, $1 bills to be specific. Once again, this is a big reason why we, as parents, need to function in some meaningful way with cash, even if not exclusively. Our children need to see us handling cash, hear us explaining the different choices we make, and have the opportunity to try it for themselves.

We often take for granted the little things like how a $5 bill is worth more than a $1 bill, but when a four-year-old gets their hands on cash we have to go back to the basics. We need to intentionally plan out how we will allow our kids to see, hear, and experience the moment-by-moment choice to follow God over money. For this, cash is the currency that makes the most sense to them.

Allowing children to put their allowance into their envelopes helps them feel a deeper connection to the plan they have made and to better understand what they are doing and why. Encouraging them to place their own order and pay the cashier themselves when they buy something allows them to truly feel responsible for their choices and purchases. Requiring them to put the money into the offering plate allows them to authentically experience the act of giving and connect their obedience to the joy of generosity.

At some point, we all have to explain to our kids how credit and debit cards work. They will naturally see us and others use them and ask us questions. We want to give accurate and intentional answers, explaining where the "money" for those cards comes from and why we sometimes use cash and other times, cards.

As kids get older, we will want to explain in greater detail the reasoning behind our personal currency choices, whatever they may be, along with the advantages and disadvantages. We may even decide to allow our kids to get their own debit, credit, or Venmo account so we can help them manage those tools responsibly when the stakes are lower.

Establishing Negotiables and Non-Negotiables

While most of the principles behind establishing negotiables and non-negotiables with our children are in line with the way we created our own, there are two unique applications I would like to discuss.

The first is using influence through a coaching mentality to lead our children to make their own good decisions. As with us, things for them will not go exactly as planned, and helping them navigate those situations are great training opportunities.

This year while Christmas shopping, our second oldest child, Barrett, found something he really wanted to get the third son, Rowan, but he didn't have enough money. So we looked some more and found another thing that would be great but, once again, he had not saved enough money. He found yet another great idea but still did not have enough money. He was pretty disheartened and stressed out. It was not that he had not saved reasonably (he had shot a little low, but not intentionally). It was just that the things Rowan would *really* like were just a couple dollars more than he had expected.

At this point, I pulled Barrett out of the toy aisle so he could focus on what I was saying as we talked through some options. The first option was that he could use some of his spending money to cover the difference. The second option was that he could move money from another gift envelope but not one of the Christmas envelopes. That would allow him to buy Rowan one of the gifts he would really like and give him time to replenish the envelope he pulled from. He countered by asking if he could just spend less on one of the other kids for Christmas. I told him he could look for other gifts, but I would decide whether he was just being cheap, or if they were gifts the recipient would enjoy even though they happened to be under budget. Sure enough, Barrett was able to find a few things Eden would genuinely enjoy for a few dollars under what he had planned. I finished off the trip by telling him he did a great job working through the problem and suggested he increase his savings target a few dollars next year.

The second unique application is that we will likely need to set some ground rules for them from time to time rather than exclusively allowing them to set their own. While our primary goal is to leverage our influence, there are times we need to exercise our control as parents.

With our spouse, there will be very few times we plant our flag and say, "I don't care what you say, we aren't doing that." But with our children, there probably *will* be some of those. Although in both cases I would encourage you to rephrase it. For many reasons.

A few years ago our kids were into Beyblades (collectible spinning top-like toys based on a Japanese cartoon). They would scour the internet looking for the rarest "blade" and spare no expense to obtain it. They would find them being sold by vendors in Asia for $50 or more with a six-week delivery date—and not even flinch. They would go with us to Walmart any time we were going so they could buy a new one—multiple times each week. We let this go on for a while, allowing them to experience the consequences of spending all their money. But when they started reducing their targeted gift savings below a reasonable level so they could increase their spending money, we had to intervene and set some limits for them. They could buy only one Beyblade each month. It could be from Asia or Walmart, $5 or $50, but only one per month. Also, they needed to get their gift envelopes up to a certain level or let their siblings know they weren't planning on getting them anything. Things pretty well stabilized after that and returned to normal. We would have preferred to let them learn the lesson on their own, but we needed to make sure reasonable boundaries were put in place in an area they were not self-regulating well.

Accountability Partners
There are three ways we can build the concept of accountability partners into discipling our children. The first is to allow them to be present in our conversations with *our* accountability partners. By allowing them to see us seeking counsel and hear us discussing financial matters with our spouse and trusted advisors, they grow more comfortable with the concept of asking for help—and to do it with a focus on godly counsel. It also gives us the opportunity to explain the value of wise counsel and why we trust whom we trust.

The second way is to be their wise counsel. By offering, or even requiring, a robust two-way discussion before significant changes to their budget or major spending decisions, you can show them the value of accountability partners.

Go in with an open mind, both challenging and encouraging them from a biblical perspective. If your goal appears to them to be nothing more than poking holes in their plan or they believe you are basing your judgment solely on your own opinions, they will learn a lesson opposite to what you intend. As with our accountability partners, the ultimate decision should be theirs whenever reasonable. Our intention is to offer counsel for them to consider and learn from.

The third way is to use *them* as *our* accountability partners. Asking them to help you think through the costs and benefits of significant decisions, both ones that directly affect them and ones that do not, will do more to make them feel included and engaged than anything else you can do in this area. It will also make them more receptive to you being *their* accountability partner.

Explaining to them what you are thinking about—and why—invites them into your life in a way they do not expect, allowing them to directly witness, understand, and challenge your decision-making criteria. As with any other accountability partner, their opinion is not binding, but the dialogue will have an incredible impact on their financial, relational, and spiritual development.

Benchmarks and Goals

As with our own benchmarks and goals, the "When we . . . we will . . ." exercise is a great way to establish expectations and contingency plans with children ("When I . . . I will . . .." for them). Some examples for them might be:

- When I have filled all my gift envelopes, I will start saving for vacation souvenirs.
- When I get money for my birthday, I will tithe, then use half of the rest to fill envelopes and half for spending.
- When I break something and have to pay for it, I will use spending money first, then vacation souvenir money, then pull from the gift envelopes that are furthest out in time.
- When I have less than $5 of spending money, I will not buy anything.

If your kids are younger or are not quite understanding what to do, you can help them by filling out the "When I . . ." part and having them come up with ideas for the "I will . . .." part. Try to leverage influence rather than control when you can. If your child decides that when they get three dollars they will buy a pony, gently redirect them by suggesting they start a pony-buying envelope. Also explain that the higher priority items need to be filled first.

When our thirteen-year-old was eight, he decided he wanted to buy a $225 hoverboard. We talked him through the cost and some of the negotiables and non-negotiables and turned him loose. Four months later, he had his $225 hoverboard! He had put the first things first, worked and saved diligently, and learned the value of enjoying God's abundant blessing!

Adjusting Mid-Week

Younger children will not have many mid-week adjustments since they generally do not have weekly expenses, but including them in conversations about yours can have a significant impact on their understanding of the process.

As kids get older, they will have car and phone expenses they will need to work through. In all cases, be positive and productive with them and help them process the decision well. This includes times when they have a financial crisis and you not only need to help them resolve it but also to review the decisions that may have led to the crisis. Fall back on the basic principles you established in creating their budget and their "When I . . . I will . . .." plans.

Don't let a bad day become a bad month. And don't let today's issue poison their long-term attitude toward learning and applying biblical financial principles. We all stumble and fall, but as Romans 5:3-5 teaches us, our suffering produces perseverance, and perseverance produces character, and our character, hope!

Although we might prefer our children to execute their God-glorifying plans perfectly on their first attempt, we should be encouraged that they are learning from their mistakes early, while the consequences are smaller. This positions them to bring even greater glory to God as an adult.

CLOSING THOUGHTS

To bring this chapter to a close, I once again want to remind us of where we started. We know God owns it all, and we have surrendered our finances back to Him by aligning our spending with His priorities. Now, we must choose. God or money. It is not a choice we make once, but one we must make moment by moment, day after day. Through the good days and the bad. Our children will be witnesses of our choices, learning each time the way *they* should go.

THREE BIGGEST TAKEAWAYS FROM THIS CHAPTER

1)

2)

3)

CHAPTER 12

Multiplication

"But the seed falling on good soil refers to someone who hears the word and understands it. This is the one who produces a crop, yielding a hundred, sixty or thirty times what was sown."

MATTHEW 13:23

The fourth Pillar of Financial Discipleship is Multiplication, the expectation and commitment to use all we've been entrusted with to grow God's kingdom. I believe there are two basic reasons why we fall short of God's instruction to *"go and make disciples"* (Matthew 28:19). First, we have a tendency to be self-focused rather than God- or others-focused. We pay close attention to the instruction to *"take the plank out of your own eye"* but miss the *reason* Jesus gives, *"and then you will see clearly to remove the speck from your brother's eye"* (Matthew 7:5).

Second, we don't feel like we know enough yet. We don't feel ready to answer the questions someone might ask or defend Scripture if someone doesn't agree. We feel like we just need a little more training or practice before we're ready to teach. With all this in mind, though, we as followers of Jesus need to recognize Scripture's clear expectation that we *will* make disciples.

The parable from which our anchor verse comes teaches us

about the requirement of multiplication in the life of a Christian. The parable of the sower found in Matthew 13 recounts:

> That same day Jesus went out of the house and sat by the lake. Such large crowds gathered around him that he got into a boat and sat in it, while all the people stood on the shore. Then he told them many things in parables, saying: "A farmer went out to sow his seed. As he was scattering the seed, some fell along the path, and the birds came and ate it up. Some fell on rocky places, where it did not have much soil. It sprang up quickly, because the soil was shallow. But when the sun came up, the plants were scorched, and they withered because they had no root. Other seed fell among thorns, which grew up and choked the plants. Still other seed fell on good soil, where it produced a crop—a hundred, sixty or thirty times what was sown. Whoever has ears, let them hear."

Coming from an agrarian culture, Jesus' audience would have been very comfortable with this story. In fact, it seems they were a little *too* comfortable with this story, as they had no clue what the parable meant. His disciples asked Him later what He was trying to teach the crowd. To them, what Jesus had said was just a story with no point. Jesus explains its meaning in verses 18-23.

> "Listen then to what the parable of the sower means: When anyone hears the message about the kingdom and does not understand it, the evil one comes and snatches away what was sown in their heart. This is the seed sown along the path. The seed falling on rocky ground refers to someone who hears the word and at once receives it with joy. But since they have no root, they last only a short time. When trouble or persecution comes because of the word, they quickly fall away. The seed falling among the thorns refers to someone who hears the word, but the worries of this life and the deceitfulness of wealth choke the word, making it unfruitful. But the seed falling on good soil refers to someone who hears the word and

understands it. This is the one who produces a crop, yielding a hundred, sixty or thirty times what was sown."

The first soil is hardpacked and unreceptive. The truth of God is shared with them and has little to no impact. The second soil is rocky and has some major limitations and deficiencies. The truth of God is shared with them, resulting in early growth that quickly dies when things get tough. The third soil is fertile and good for growing but is corrupted by priorities that aren't consistent with God's. The truth of God grows but the growth is unfruitful and produces no harvest. Finally, the fourth soil is "good" and not only grows but produces exponential fruit, seed that can be planted again for more fruit.

There's a lot we could unpack in this, but I'll point out one truth, then focus in on a second. Notice the difference between soils two and three. The second soil fails because of hardship while the third soil fails because of wealth. The second soil loses sight of what's important because of a perceived lack, while the third soil is distracted by the false comforts of life. Let that soak in.

The more relevant truth to consider for our purpose is that the production of fruit is what makes the fourth soil "good" and the third soil not good. As we established earlier, "good" means fulfilling its purpose. If the only soil that is judged "good" by Jesus is the only one that multiplied, we can only conclude that Jesus equates our purpose with multiplication. Soil one didn't grow at all. Soil two grew but didn't last long. Soils three and four both grew and stayed alive, but only soil four reproduced. According to this parable, our soil (lives) can be rich and lush with all kinds of potential for leafy greens and beautifully adorned flowers, but if we don't create a next generation of plants, we fail. As followers of Jesus, we *must* multiply.

MULTIPLICATION IN OUR LIVES

Unfortunately, we tend to overthink and overcomplicate the idea of multiplication. We make it into some big undertaking and event, get intimidated, and go back into our shells. We think it means going door to door handing out tracts, starting an after-school program at the public school, or going to seminary to be properly educated. Those things are good, and if that's where God is leading you, do it. For most of us, though, it will (and should) be much simpler and more organic. Here are three basic ways we, as followers of Jesus, can multiply for kingdom impact.

MVP Parenting

The good news is that the whole point of this book is to help you multiply your faith, knowledge, and experience! The entire premise of learning and applying godly financial principles to teach your children is multiplication. By providing Modeling, Verbal Instruction, and Practical Opportunities, you will be creating a harvest for the King that He can then replant to further grow His kingdom.

As you've already learned, you don't need be an expert at something to pass it along. When Andrew invited his brother Simon to meet Jesus, the only thing he knew was that Jesus was the Messiah (John 1:41). That's it. Notice, Andrew didn't need to go to special school before sharing what he knew. No tracts to guide him or certification program to complete. He had only been with Jesus for one day!

Likewise, you don't know much about budgeting yet, but you know enough to tell your children about it. You know enough to get started on your budget and help them start theirs. You know enough to model humility by saying, "Let's learn how to budget together," and to explain that we don't need to be experts to help others.

By applying the MVP Parenting model, you are obeying Jesus' command to make disciples. You *are* growing His kingdom. Even more exciting, as we take an active approach to discipling our children and others, we grow in our relationship with God and establish this type of faithfulness for our children's baseline as they grow into adults. Although many of us were surprised to learn later in life that multiplication was an expectation of all followers of Jesus—not just pastors and missionaries—our children will know this fact from the start.

Sharing and Discussing

The next way you can multiply God's kingdom is to intentionally share what you've read or watched and discuss it with others. In 2015, I was a pretty nominal Christian. We were a part of an extremely healthy church where faith was prepared and served with little to no effort on our part. I was a weekly church attender, a consistent tither, and an occasional Sunday School Class leader. I was learning a lot, but I wasn't all-in, and certainly wasn't multiplying.

Then we relocated for my job and entered a dark chapter of our walk with Christ. God called us to a church that was not healthy, giving us an opening to share what we had learned. But the things we had been accustomed to weren't in place and the vast majority of the church had no desire to see them put in place. So we got stagnant. We continued attending church and tithing, trying to swim upstream to make a difference, but we weren't even growing, let alone multiplying. Work was frustrating. Our kids were frustrating. Our faith was frustrating. It was all frustrating.

Then a friend who was in a similar situation invited me to do the One More program with him through Compass. Like me, he was a corporate guy who had relocated. His family hadn't found the right church home yet and he needed something to push him. In some ways it was the blind leading the blind (Matthew 15:14). In other ways, iron sharpening iron (Proverbs 27:17). Either way, it took my faith from stagnant to supercharged in that one year, a pace I've maintained since.

The model was simple and highly repeatable. Read a couple chapters each week and get together every two weeks to discuss. No formal worksheets or packets. No teachers or students. Just a couple of friends learning together. And don't forget the coffee.

Now I do the same with friends from church, friends from work, my wife, my kids, and anyone else God puts in my path. It doesn't need to be any particular book. I just never read a book alone. If I find a book I want to read, I invite someone to read it with me. If I watch a video on YouTube that I find challenging or encouraging, I share it with someone and follow up by texting my reflections and asking theirs. It almost seems too simple, but it's been one of the most impactful and organic ways of growing God's kingdom and His community of believers.

If you aren't already doing something like this, consider reading this book again with your spouse or a friend. Chapter by chapter discuss what was impactful, what you agreed with, what you disagreed with, what questions you still have, and anything else that comes up. In doing so, you will grow your perspective, your relationship, and His kingdom.

Sharing Your Testimony

The third way we can incorporate multiplication into our personal walk with Christ is to follow Peter's instruction given in 1 Peter 3:15, "... *Always be prepared to give an answer to everyone who asks you to give the reason for the hope that you have.*" I know I promised to offer only simple ways to multiply, and this doesn't seem simple, but it's not as complicated as it seems. "Sharing your testimony" means telling your story. If there's anything you actually *are* an expert about, it's your own life.

Applied literally, we are taught to know and be prepared to share the reason we have faith and hope in Jesus. Every believer has a story of who they were and who they are, connected by something that happened. I walked away from God and returned when three different Christians in three different stages of my life showed me the unconditional love of Christ. I was in financial ruin because of poor choices but was restored to a position of stability and contentment because of what God's word teaches about money and possessions. My faith was stagnant but is now supercharged because I learned to learn with other believers. Each is a simple way of connecting where I was to where I am by something that happened.

Sharing our stories, however, doesn't have to be a prepared speech or dissertation. 2 Corinthians 1:3-5 tells us that the comfort we have received from God can be used to comfort others going through similar experiences.

We often speak of "sympathy" and "empathy," but I think understanding the difference is important here. Sympathy is our ability to *know* how another person feels, while empathy is our ability to *feel* how another person feels. Sympathy is a very good thing and allows us to minister to people and meet their needs. Empathy, however, allows us to actually relate to the person and meet their spiritual, emotional, and relational needs at a much deeper level.

Being able to listen to what someone is going through and say, "I have been through something similar and here's what I learned," offers incredible comfort and hope—and the only thing you have to share is your own experience. No deep theology or scientific research, only Spirit-filled perspective from a person who has been there before.

This applies to both good times and bad. What did you go through? What hurt and what helped? As we help others, we don't want to change the subject from their experience to ours, but we can engage at a deeper level when we allow ourselves to be vulnerable.

We all want intimacy in our lives. We want to be known and understood deeply by others. Unfortunately, intimacy is built on trust, and trust is something we are cautious about giving out. Even harder, trust is built on vulnerability, which gives others the opportunity to hurt us, something we guard closely. By sharing our own experiences, we extend trust to someone who needs to be able to trust. We set an example for them to follow, opening the door to sharing God's truth with them when they need it most.

This applies to all aspects of life, including finances. As we've established before, talking about money is taboo in our culture. But offering help in this culturally sensitive area amplifies and multiplies the impact it can have in a relationship. High risk can deliver high reward if we are willing to follow Jesus' example and meet people's needs through our own vulnerability.

MULTIPLICATION IN OUR CHILDREN'S LIVES

Just Being Kids

In many ways, kids have a significant advantage over adults in the area of multiplication. Jesus points out some of their natural advantages at the beginning of Matthew 18. When asked who is the greatest in the kingdom of heaven (verse 1), He calls over a child (verse 2) and says, *"Truly I tell you, unless you change and become like little children, you will never enter the kingdom of heaven. Therefore, whoever takes the lowly position of this child is the greatest in the kingdom of heaven. And whoever welcomes one such child in my name welcomes me"* (verses 3-5). Children are humble, open-minded, and pliable. They lack those "boxes" we talked about earlier and put aside the skepticism that becomes prevalent in adults.

They have a structured social setting in school, talk more openly, and care more authentically. The bar for being considered a "friend" is generally much lower for kids than adults, but they share their lives as deeply with their "friends" as adults do. Eden, our four-year-old, considers anyone she talks with to be her "friend." She doesn't even know their name, and never did, but they are still a friend. And if you're her "friend," she'll tell you about her family, her preschool, and her church. She doesn't even think twice.

Helping our kids channel these skills can be an incredible tool of evangelism. A friend of mine has a kindergartener we can all learn from. When he meets someone for the first time, one of his first questions of them is always, "Do you know Jesus?" Afterward, he brings it up to his parents and elaborates on the person's answer. If they said they know Jesus, he wonders where they go to church. If they said they don't, he wants to invite them to church. It, no doubt, makes many of the adults uncomfortable, but it plants a seed and allows the Spirit to go to work on the person. Our kids can't accurately determine who is a Soil 1, 2, 3, or 4 any better than we can, but they can scatter the seed as we're all called to do.

Inviting Others

Children's willingness and enthusiasm for inviting other kids to activities is another natural way kids can grow God's kingdom. Our kids are constantly asking if friends can come over after school and on the weekends, have sleepovers, and go to the trampoline park. Well, they can also be encouraged to invite kids to come to church. For children, any time together has value and, while they would probably rather hang out at the trampoline park, they will also value time together at church.

Our oldest son is a great salesman. I remember when he did his first fundraiser for school and was peddling over-priced food items at a church social function. He came back and told us how much he had sold and, trying to be a godly parent, I asked him how he responds when someone doesn't want to buy anything. He stared at me blankly and said, "No one ever says no." He's carried this mentality into his evangelism, and with great results. He's invited kids, adults, and families to church, groups, and Bible studies. Many accept his invitation, whether out of interest or guilt.

Now 13, he has made friends with another young man, Nathan, down the street and has gotten him involved in our church's Youth Group. Nathan's family doesn't attend church and he had never even been inside one (as far as he can remember). During the summer, the Youth Group met every week, going through a short devotional and discussion, followed by some sort of fun activity. Nathan went to these meetings consistently but never joined us on Sundays or accepted salvation (as far as we know).

This fall, Weston invited him to go out to dinner with us. We have a nightly tradition that Eden picks who prays. There's occasional grumbling, but we generally respect her authority in the matter and abide by her rulings. As you would guess, Eden's pick for that night was Nathan. He was visibly uncomfortable with the idea, so I offered him the option to pass.

"I'll do it," he said, "but I don't really know what I'm supposed to say."

"Well, start with 'God,'" I said, "and end with 'Amen,' and say what's on your mind in between."

His prayer was simple, thanking God for the food and friends. But it was a big deal. It was probably the first time he'd ever spoken directly to God, and almost certainly the first time he'd done it in public. All because Weston invited him and Eden called on him.

Nathan still hasn't joined us on Sundays or accepted salvation (as far as we know), but the seed is planted and the Spirit's at work.

Helping Siblings and Other Kids

The final way for children to grow God's kingdom is for them to help train their siblings and other kids. Just as we demonstrated financial faithfulness, explained the "whats" and "whys" to our children, and offered them opportunities to try it themselves, we have also been modeling discipleship to them. As our kids get older, we can encourage them to disciple each other, both in their finances and in general.

A friend of mine has seven boys (yeah), and I had asked him about how they and their church disciple their youth. He told me that their church had an amazing program, but he wanted a couple of his kids to explain it to me instead. The next time I was in the area, I went over to their house and had a chance to sit down with three of them.

The oldest in the group was 19 and had been discipled by one of the Youth Group leaders. He, in turn, had started discipling the 16-year-old, who began discipling the 14-year-old. Similar to the model I described earlier, the church had selected a seven-module resource that walked the group through basic theology from salvation through discipleship. None of those kids, including the 19-year-old, had all the answers, but they had more answers than their younger sibling, and they were willing to share.

In the same way, our older kids can help our younger kids with their budgets. They can share their own stories of success and stumbles. They aren't experts in the field of Christian finances, but they know enough to share.

Start by introducing the idea and coaching them up for it. "You've done a good job with your budgeting, and I'd like to have you help your brother with his." Follow that with some additional direction such as, "I'd really like you to help him plan out his gift savings like you've done. I'm not as concerned about the vacation savings and those things, but you've done a good job preparing for the gift expenses and I think he would get a lot out of your guidance." This is textbook biblical discipleship: we train someone to train someone to train someone.

CLOSING THOUGHTS

Most of us, myself included, feel ill-equipped and unprepared to go out and make disciples, but we need to remember Jesus' final instructions in Matthew 28:18-20. "... *All authority in heaven and on earth has been given to me. Therefore go and make disciples of all nations, baptizing them in the name of the Father and of the Son and of the Holy Spirit, and teaching them to obey everything I have commanded you. And surely I am with you always, to the very end of the age."*

All authority belongs to Him and He instructs us to go out and make disciples. He tells us to teach them to obey all that He has commanded. And He tells us He will be with us always.

Multiplication doesn't have to be complex. We don't need special training or an advanced degree in theology. We simply need to be passionate about the mission Jesus has given us and be open and responsive to His Spirit. After all, He is with us always, even to the very end of the age.

THREE BIGGEST TAKEAWAYS FROM THIS CHAPTER

1)

2)

3)

CHAPTER 13

Eternal Focus

*"Those who are victorious will inherit all this,
and I will be their God and they will
be my children."*

REVELATION 21:7

The fifth Pillar of Financial Discipleship, Eternal Focus, serves as a compass for our efforts to become faithful financial disciples, guiding our application of the first four Pillars. As we and our families establish principles and practices that align our finances to God's priorities, we need to ensure two things: first, that our goal is clearly defined and kept front-of-mind; second, that our actions lead to that goal.

In his book *Pursuit of Holiness*[13], Jerry Bridges helps readers reconcile the biblical mandate to be holy (Leviticus 11:44) with our inevitable failure through sin (Romans 3:23). Bridges correctly points out that although we will certainly fail, the constant struggle to be holy demonstrates our commitment to God and, through perseverance, actually leads us toward our goal. The consistent failures on the way serve as reminders that our sinful nature won't give up the fight easily and that intentional and persistent effort is required to grow in likeness to Jesus. He says the key to progress in this pursuit will not be through a mere concession of our vices but in an alignment of our wills. "Before we can *act* we must *will*. To will means to desire and to resolve."

As our anchor verse points out, this battle of wills, fought throughout our lives, doesn't impact just our life on earth but also our life throughout eternity.

This chapter was by far the most difficult chapter for me to write. Well, that's not entirely true. It was so easy I have actually half-written it three times now, this being the fourth. What's been difficult, however, has been creating something informative, challenging, motivational, and actionable.

The truth is, the entire Bible is a reminder to maintain eternal focus, to put aside the things of this world in order to achieve the things of the next. It's a story about God creating us, selecting us, adopting us, saving us, and redeeming us so that we can be with Him for all of eternity. It is a collection of writings that document the path from the temporal to the eternal.

Each time I wrote, I ironically lost my focus. There is so much to say about the topic that versions one through three ended up being data-dumps. Like the spray of a power-washer into the air, what started as a powerful, focused thought kept resulting in a vague mist. Without significant and intentional effort, we will find our lives resulting in the same.

As previously established, our goal in life is simple: grow in relationship with—and likeness to—Jesus, glorifying God with everything He has entrusted to us.

We cannot lose our focus. Successfully applying Pillars one through four will have no impact if they are not focused on achieving this goal. We may achieve the world's goals of freedom from debt, financial stability, a comfortable retirement, and leaving an inheritance to our children's children, but we won't achieve our true goal if we aren't focused on eternity. As our anchor verse reminds us, the stakes are high, eternally high. If we are faithful and overcome the obstacles of this world, the reward will be amazing and well worth the fight.

FAILURES OF WORLDLY WEALTH

Scripture offers many examples of how worldly wealth and pursuits will fail us. It also provides many reasons why. I will focus on just three.

Worldly Wealth is Meaningless

When I was a new Christian and resolved to read the Bible from beginning to end, the first book that really grabbed my attention was Ecclesiastes. The first 20 books were fine, but I was reading them wrong, so they didn't have the impact they *should* have—and later *would* have. I was making the same general mistakes many new Christians make, reading it slowly and viewing it as a divine instruction manual. (If this is how you're currently reading the Bible, I recommend you read *How to Read the Bible for All Its Worth* and/or use *BibleProject* videos to help you engage at a deeper level.)

The opening lines of Ecclesiastes, however, caught me off guard.

> *The words of the Teacher, son of David, king in Jerusalem:*
> *"Meaningless! Meaningless!" says the Teacher. "Utterly meaningless! Everything is meaningless."*

This was unexpected, to say the least. The last thing I expected to read in the Bible was how meaningless everything was. I expected the Bible to tell me all about how meaning-FULL everything was! God had my attention.

The next 12 chapters detail all the things the author had found to be meaningless: wisdom, pleasure, folly, work, oppression, success, riches, obedience, poverty, and about every other detail of life you can think of—until the conclusion of the book in chapter 12, verses 13-14:

> Now all has been heard; here is the conclusion of the matter: Fear God and keep his commandments, for this is the duty of all mankind. For God will bring every deed into judgment, including every hidden thing, whether it is good or evil.

This is still one of my favorite books and I make a point of always reading it in one sitting. That is the best way to read all books of the Bible, but especially Ecclesiastes. The introduction (Ecclesiastes 1:1-2) presents an issue or problem; the body (Ecclesiastes 1:3-12:8) elaborates on that problem; and the conclusion (Ecclesiastes 12:9-14) resolves the issue.

We must be extremely careful about pulling any specific verse or passage out of the middle of this book—and do our due diligence when we see someone else doing it. There are too many misdirects and reversals to haphazardly pluck a single gem out of the middle in verse-of-the-day style. More than likely, you will find later that you missed the point entirely. I concede that it is certainly possible to strategically pull excerpts from the middle and preserve the true meaning in its context, but this book, more than most, is easy to misapply.

The beauty of this book is that it establishes a problem we all face: the day-to-day pursuits of our life often seem meaningless. This is the feeling most of us get when we achieve our worldly goals and still feel unsatisfied.

Solomon goes to great lengths to ensure that his book is relatable to absolutely any reader. Whether you are wise or a fool, rich or poor, in power or oppressed, beautiful or not so much, *"the Teacher"* speaks to you and your situation in life. And it clearly articulates the only thing that has meaning: pursuing the things of God, the eternal.

This book, in its entirety, makes one point: the worldly is meaningless because the eternal is the only thing that matters.

Worldly Wealth is Temporary and Contingent

The second reason worldly wealth will fail us is due to its temporary and contingent nature. Once again we can turn to Jesus' Sermon on the Mount, where He instructs His audience to *"not store up for yourselves treasures on earth, where moths and vermin destroy, and where thieves break in and steal"* (Matthew 6:19). In its literal application, Jesus points out how fragile and short-lived things of this world are. Cash currency erodes, metal currency corrodes, and both can easily be stolen or lost.

In a figurative sense, He reinforces what we learned in Ecclesiastes: worldly treasures lack real intrinsic value and are contingent on conditions and circumstances we can't control. Cash, coins, and any other thing of worldly value hold that value only as long as others also recognize their value.

Gold has been the standard of wealth for thousands of years, but if people stopped valuing it, if it became common or unattractive, any gold you owned would be worthless. Once backed by gold, the US dollar is now backed only by the decree of the government. The only thing that gives the $10 bill in your wallet or purse any value is a little statement: "This note is legal tender for all debts, public and private." If the US government lost its authority, that piece of paper would be worthless. Electronic currency, the "money" you have in a bank or investment account, only holds value as long as the bank or market recognizes its value and honors their commitment to value it.

As I write this, the scandal of the month is a man who was involved in a cryptocurrency business and lost his entire $16 billion fortune in the course of a week. I am not taking a position on cryptocurrency or the accusations made against him, but think about the simple idea that in one week $16 billion could just disappear. $16 billion! That would be like having 16,000 piles of cash on the floor, each with $1 million in it. And then it's gone! Can you imagine having that kind of money and living that kind of life—and then having it just disappear? In one week? No time to prepare. No time to prevent it. Between Monday and Friday, it's just gone. At the beginning of the week, the world valued what he had; by the end of the week, it didn't. What he possessed went from meaningful to meaningless in the world's eyes in one week.

Thankfully, the things of God cannot be taken away, and God will continue backing eternal currency. Jesus follows the instruction we looked at earlier with this: *"But store up for yourselves treasures in heaven, where moths and vermin do not destroy, and where thieves do not break in and steal"* (Matthew 6:20). The eternal treasure does not erode or corrode and cannot be stolen—even by Satan. Its intrinsic value, backed by the Creator Himself, never rises or falls. It is perfectly stable and perfectly safe.

Worldly Wealth is Frail

A third reason worldly wealth fails us is its inability to pass God's survival test. First Corinthians 3:11-15 says:

> *For no one can lay any foundation other than the one already laid, which is Jesus Christ. If anyone builds on this foundation using gold, silver, costly stones, wood, hay or straw, their work will be shown for what it is, because the Day will bring it to light. It will be revealed with fire, and the fire will test the quality of each person's work. If what has been built survives, the builder will receive a reward. If it is burned up, the builder will suffer loss but yet will be saved—even though only as one escaping through the flames.*

Paul tells us that as each of us transitions from this life to the next, the results of our life will be tested by God to determine whether they are pure or impure, worldly or eternal. If we have accepted salvation, we will be saved; but in a way I don't understand, we will suffer loss when our false treasures don't make it in with us. As God reveals what we've accomplished and why, only those things consistent with His will (built on the foundation of Christ) and dedicated to His glory (as revealed by the fire) will survive.

God expects us to accomplish His will His way. No other approach will survive. If we accomplish His will but do it our way, it will burn up. If we follow His instructions but do it for worldly reasons, it will burn up. We must accomplish His will His way—His eternal outcomes using His eternal methods.

DISTRACTIONS

Since you've made it to Chapter 13 in a book about learning and applying biblical financial principles in your home, you probably don't need much more convincing that our focus *should be* on the eternal, so let's shift over to the execution side. In Luke 4:1-13, we read about Jesus being tempted three times. I believe Satan applies the same strategy to try to distract us from the eternal focus we know we should have.

Provision

After 40 days in the wilderness without food, Satan's first appeal in verse 3 was to Jesus' need for provision. *"If you are the Son of God, tell this stone to become bread,"* he said. No doubt about it, after having nothing to eat for 40 days, Jesus was hungry and Satan knew it. He knew that Jesus' humanity would make Him susceptible to our most basic physical needs.

Most of us haven't fasted for 40 days and are not in danger of running low on food, let alone out of it, but Satan still distracts us with a fear of not having enough. He whispers lies about how giving any more will put our families at risk, how our kids won't fit in if they don't have nicer clothes, or how they won't be successful if they don't go to the right schools.

Jesus was hungry, starving in fact. He had gone 40 days without food and certainly had the ability to turn the stone into bread. But he also had a laser-sharp focus on eternity. Turning to God's word, He replies, *"It is written: 'Man shall not live on bread alone.'"* Jesus knew that if He was doing the will of His Father, He had no reason to worry about food. He could, instead, remain focused on the more important eternal matters.

As Jesus did, we need to have confidence that God can and will provide. Jesus puts the matter to rest in Matthew 6:25-34 when He says:

> *"Therefore I tell you, do not worry about your life, what you will eat or drink; or about your body, what you will wear. Is not life more than food, and the body more than clothes? Look at the birds of the air; they do not sow or reap or store away in barns, and yet your heavenly Father feeds them. Are you not much more valuable than they? Can any one of you by worrying add a single hour to your life?*
>
> *"And why do you worry about clothes? See how the flowers of the field grow. They do not labor or spin. Yet I tell you that not even Solomon in all his splendor was dressed like one of these. If that is how God clothes the grass of the field, which is here today and tomorrow is thrown into the fire, will he not much more clothe you—you of little faith? So do not worry,*

saying, 'What shall we eat?' or 'What shall we drink?' or 'What shall we wear?' For the pagans run after all these things, and your heavenly Father knows that you need them. But seek first his kingdom and his righteousness, and all these things will be given to you as well. Therefore do not worry about tomorrow, for tomorrow will worry about itself. Each day has enough trouble of its own."

God can and will provide for us based on what He knows is best for us. He may not provide what we want, but He will absolutely provide what we need. It may not be what *we* think we need from our limited perspective, but it will be what *He* knows we need from His eternal perspective.

We can have an eternal impact by being faithful with our finances and teaching our children to do the same. Like Jesus, we must not allow anxiety over basic provision to draw our eyes away from eternal reality.

Power

Next, Satan takes Jesus to a high place (generally a place of worship in Scripture) and quickly shows Him all the earth, offering Him the power to rule over it—all if Jesus will just worship him. After 40 days, Jesus no doubt felt powerless. By taking human form, He had voluntarily surrendered some part of His divine authority. He knew He had a mission to accomplish, but He also knew the cost. As bad as 40 days in the desert without food must have been, it was nothing compared to what He would have to go through on the cross to save the world.

Here was an easy way out. After all, the whole point of the cross was for the Father to pass His authority over to Jesus. Satan is just offering a quicker way to do it. If He just worshipped Satan for a few minutes, a small compromise and nothing more, He could skip the cross and get right back to doing God's work. Once Satan gave Jesus authority over the earth, He could use that authority to do good and to save souls!

Jesus, however, would not be fooled like the first Adam had been. He won't be distracted by temporary things and instead puts

Satan in his place a second time, saying in verse 8, *"It is written: 'Worship the Lord your God and serve him only.'"*

How often do we fall for this trick? The enemy suggests an easier way, and we're all ears. He whispers that we can still accomplish what God wants; we can just do it faster and without as much sacrifice. And we take the bait. He points out that it's just a small compromise; we're forgiven anyway. And we take our eyes off God.

Like Jesus, we must always turn back to God's written word, His felt presence, and the wise counsel of His devout followers to remain focused on the eternal. If we do His will His way, He will exalt us (James 4:10). All other paths lead to destruction (Matthew 7:13).

Popularity

Finally, in verse 9, Satan appeals to Jesus' human desire for validation and recognition. He dares Jesus to jump from the top of the temple, misusing God's word as he cites Psalm 91:11-12, *"For it is written: 'He will command his angels concerning you to guard you carefully; they will lift you up in their hands, so that you will not strike your foot against a stone.'"*

We all have the desire to be known and accepted. Jesus, in human form, was no different. Having been born in a stable, raised as a carpenter's son, seen as just an average kid to most, and nearly starved after 40 days alone in the desert, Jesus wants people to know who He is and what He has been sent to do. Satan simply offers Him that chance.

The temple Satan wants Jesus to jump from isn't some backwoods church. This is THE temple. There would have been thousands of people around to witness it, to immediately know Jesus was the promised Son of God sent to save the world. It would have been an amazing way to begin Jesus' ministry and establish His authority.

But Jesus knows better. He responds in verse 12, *"It is said: 'Do not put the Lord your God to the test.'"* The Father's plan is the only one that matters.

Again, we must have the same laser focus on eternity and not be distracted by the lure of popularity. Theodore Roosevelt is often quoted as saying that comparison is the thief of joy, and I think it is because comparison interferes with contentment. As we compare what we have or don't have to what others have or don't have, we wind up dissatisfied with what God has given us. My old car seems fine until I find out they make a new model with heated seats. My paycheck seems fine until I find out what my coworker makes. My house seems fine until I see one with an extra bedroom and a little more land for sale.

Rather than comparing what God has provided for us with what He has provided for others, we need to ask the simple question, "Is what I have enough to do what God has called me to do?" The answer, of course, is yes. As envy and jealousy begin to boil up again and again, we need to ask that same question again and again, reminding ourselves again and again that God has provided us with what we need in order to accomplish what He has called us to do. He may provide more, but never less.

Some have been given nice things, and lots of them, to do God's work (David and Solomon). Others have been given just barely enough (John the Baptist and Jesus). Some in our day will be given amazing platforms for their ministries. Others will be given opportunities that will never make the newspaper or Twitter, like discipling our kids at home.

Whatever our specific calling, we must remain focused on the eternal outcomes of the path God has called us to. We must continue taking steps (large or small) in that direction, turning neither to the right nor the left (Proverbs 4:27).

CLOSING THOUGHTS

Once we have successfully focused our eyes on the eternal, there is one final challenge to seeing it through. We must persevere.

Erica reminded me of this one night, after an especially tough day with the kids. I don't remember the details, but they had joined forces and fought against some basic request I had made. It could have been brushing teeth, taking baths or showers, putting on pajamas, changing underwear twice in the same week (heaven forbid), the consumption of vegetables at dinner, or any number of other things we battle as parents every day. But on this day, I surrendered. Erica asked me what happened and why they weren't doing what we normally require. I don't remember any of the details except for the simple conversation. I said, "I'm tired of fighting them over this. It's not worth it."

Her response was a stark reminder of the calling of a parent. She said simply, "Yes, it is."

She was right. I had lost my focus on the eternal. In that moment of frustration, I took my eyes off why we do what we do, why we require what we require. Every time I'm tempted to give up, temporarily or permanently, I remember her words and God's promises.

None of what we've covered in this book so far is easy, but it is absolutely worth it. Imagine for a moment your kids growing into adults who fully and freely serve God. Adults who glorify God in all they do. With their time, their talents, and their money. As a parent, the only thing better than hearing Jesus say to us, *"Well done, good and faithful servant. Enter into the joy of your Master,"* will be hearing Jesus say it to our kids.

The same things that tempted Jesus tempt us, and the same things that tempt us will tempt our children. By training them to anticipate these temptations, to identify the lies of Satan when they hear them, and to bring their focus back to the eternal, we offer them an incredible advantage in their lives.

Recognizing that God owns it all is a hard pill to swallow. Surrendering it all back to Him demands humility and trust. Aligning our spending to God's priorities requires significant compromise. Choosing God over money necessitates discipline. Teaching our children to do the same will take incredible patience. But it's worth it!

In those moments of our lives when we want to give in or give up—the moments when we want to take the easy way out—we need to think about that moment when our kids stand before Jesus, with us in the background, and hear those amazing words, *"Enter into the joy of your Master."*

THREE BIGGEST TAKEAWAYS FROM THIS CHAPTER

1)

2)

3)

PART 4

Finishing Touches

CHAPTER 14

Outside Influences

> *Therefore if you have any encouragement from being united with Christ, if any comfort from his love, if any common sharing in the Spirit, if any tenderness and compassion, then make my joy complete by being like-minded, having the same love, being one in spirit and of one mind.*
>
> PHILIPPIANS 2:1-2

As we've seen, we have an incredible and unavoidable influence on our children. Whether we engage or disengage, explain or ignore, MVP Parent or nothing, we influence our kids. In learning to embrace this fact, we use it to our and our children's advantage. We begin to intentionally choose the influence we will have. We choose to engage, explain, and MVP Parent. We recognize the strategy as the long game that it is, encouraging our kids to grow a little at a time in the direction we intend.

While our influence is greater than just about anyone else's in our children's lives, there are thousands of other individuals who will also influence them—some intentionally good, others intentionally bad, and still others who have no plan at all.

In this chapter, I will share some best practices for working with and around some of these outside influences, especially those whose influence does not train our children in the way we want them to go.[14]

Like everything else in the Christian walk, there are few cut-and-dried answers. To determine how to best handle the situations of life, we need to turn to God's written word, the voice of His Spirit, and the wise counsel of His people.

Though the Bible does not provide us a clean outline for this type of conflict resolution, the best practices I suggest can be found throughout the Epistles in the New Testament, especially those of the apostle Paul as he works through significant issues with grace and love without compromising his ideals.

PRAY

We are probably all susceptible to the "Lord, I pray you help this person get his mind right and quit being a jerk," kind of prayer. Most of us tend toward this even more when our children's well-being is involved. We know it isn't the kind of praying for our enemy Jesus instructs in Matthew 5:44, but it's definitely what's on our hearts in the moment. In contrast, Paul consistently opened and closed most of his letters by offering grace and love to his audience.

Here are some specific things you can pray for when you prepare to address these situations. Praying for ourselves as well as the person on the other side of the conversation, we pray:

- That we would remain focused on the eternal goals, not our personal preferences.
- That we would be open-minded to the perspectives of others.
- That we would truly seek to understand and preserve or reconcile relationships.
- That we would express our love for our children in a way that attracts others to Jesus.
- That we would have clear discernment of God's will and plans.
- That we would model to our children a healthy approach to conflict resolution.
- That the other person would be drawn into a deeper relationship with Jesus.

- That the other person would see our love for our children and our commitment to providing, protecting, and preparing them.
- That the other person would be blessed with abundance in every area of their life.

SEEK TO UNDERSTAND

After praying, the first step we should take when we recognize someone's influence over our children is to seek to understand. We see in the Epistles that Paul never wrote without first understanding what was going on in a church and why. Though he never says it specifically, he was clearly very patient and left his pen in its place until he had a deep understanding of the underlying issues a church or community was dealing with. As we manage the various influences in our kids' lives, we should try to learn what these individuals believe, the influence their beliefs are having, and the motivations behind their influence.

Their beliefs include everything from their big-picture worldview to the best way to execute that worldview. Our kids will be influenced by all of this. Are they Christian, Muslim, agnostic? Do they believe God gave us money so we could spend it, or do they believe it should be neither seen nor talked about? Is secular music the work of the devil or "just music"? Again, we are seeking to understand, not pass judgment or cut off all exposure. If we shun every person who doesn't see the world the way we do, we will miss out on many opportunities to share the gospel.

Next, we need to determine the kind of influence they're having. Specifically, do they have a lot of influence or a little, and is our child turned toward or away from the person's example. Friends, teachers, and grandparents (more on grandparents later) have the greatest impact, but kids on their soccer team have impact as well. Likewise, our kids can be influenced both toward or away from someone else's beliefs and behaviors. We may be concerned because of the clothes a new friend wears only to finds their choice in clothing is unappealing to our child.

Finally, we want to understand their motives. For parents, family, teachers, and friends, they are probably doing what they are doing out of love. We may not agree with their worldview or the way they express it, but their goal is likely to bring joy to our kids. This is a good thing. Others, however, may actually be out to harm our kids, intentionally or unintentionally.

How we manage these outside influences will vary as widely as our responses to these three basic questions (what these individuals believe, the influence their beliefs are having, and motivations behind their influence).

If we find a strong Christian has developed a strong rapport with one of our children, we should embrace and lean into this. Allow them to supplement our own influence, and encourage them to spend time together.

If a person is dragging our kids down, we will want to steer the relationship in a healthier direction or put up barriers to minimize the damage they may cause.

FIND COMMON GROUND

The next step in managing outside influences is to find common ground. In most cases, if we peel back their motives or methods far enough, we will find something we have in common that we can appeal to and build from. Paul's letters repeatedly emphasized the common ground he shared with his audience by appealing to their faith in Jesus and reminding them of the things they had been taught (Romans 1:5-7, 1 Corinthians 1:10).

Like Paul, it's important we work to find and articulate our common ground. Do they have our Christian goals but a different plan for how to get there? Are they Christian but want to make sure their kids live comfortably? Are they agnostic in their faith and indifferent toward the handling of money but believe volunteering is important? In almost all cases there is some common ground that can provide a beginning point. It is ideal if it's something significant like faith in Christ, but a favorite football team is at least something.

Let's look at a parent outside our home as an example. You want to teach your children to be faithful followers of Jesus, bringing glory to Him through their responsible handling of money. Their dad, on the other hand, isn't a Christian and doesn't think the kids need to be worried about money at all. He makes a good income, saves for retirement, their college, and spends a lot of quality time with them. We should begin by respecting their significant parental influence, and rightly so.

We see, though, that their position stands in stark opposition to what we want for our children. We need to find common ground. More than likely, their dad has taken his position out of love, based on his own experiences and how he's been influenced. If that's the case, appealing to the shared love you have for your kids is a great place to start. If, on the other hand, his position is based on apathy and a disinterest, you may need to appeal to his desire for independence and freedom.

BUILD RAPPORT

Once we have found common ground, we can begin to establish our own relationship and rapport with the outside influence. This can be seen in the Epistles by noticing that Paul frequently references some level of relationship with each church he writes to. Whenever possible, he had personally visited the churches (Rome, Corinth, Galatia, Ephesus, Philippi, and Thessalonica) and referenced those visits in his letters to remind them of their shared experiences.

When he doesn't have visits to reference (Colossae), he (a) reminds them often of their shared faith (Colossians 1:2-14), (b) relies heavily on referencing the people he personally knows in the community (Colossians 4:7-9), and (c) articulates the details of conflict in the church (listed and addressed throughout the letter). Paul's original audience, whether they liked or agreed with the points he was making, would have felt a personal connection to him and would have been more open to his message because of it.

As you engage with people who are influencing your children, if you don't agree on the big stuff, you need to take a step back and build a relationship on smaller stuff. If the person is a strong Christian, you can talk to them about their faith before bringing up the way they are influencing your children. If they aren't a Christian, you can talk with them about their hobbies and interests. We are all more likely to listen to another person and truly engage in a conversation if we believe the person cares about us. Even if the conversation is somewhat superficial, it can help establish your own influence with that person.

If your child develops a strong relationship with a friend from school, make a point of spending time with them. Whether you invite them over for dinner or just talk with them when you're giving them a ride, actively engage and show interest in them and their life.

People generally like talking about themselves and their interests. The easiest way to build rapport with just about anyone is to ask them questions and actually listen to their answers. When you genuinely care about the person, you will not only be in a better position to help your child and to influence this person toward Christ but you will also develop a deeper love for that person as you recognize that they too are a child of God made in His image.

EXPLAIN AND APPEAL

Once you feel that you understand the person's influence, position, and motives, you have a basis for finding common ground and building rapport. With that in place, you can now, if appropriate, directly address a conflict and seek resolution.

Paul, in all his letters, thoroughly explained the problem(s) and invited the audience into the solution. He spoke harshly sometimes and softly at others but always explained the issue, the implications, and the correct solution.

No matter who the person is, we want to show them love and respect, point out the common ground, directly tie our appeal to that common ground, and then ask for their help. No one likes to be told what to do; being invited in as part of the solution will be much more effective than giving instructions (influence rather than control).

Let's go back again to the parent-outside-the-home scenario. If the parent is not a Christian but deeply loves and cares for their children and doesn't think money should be talked about, the conversation could begin like this: "We both love our kids and want them to be healthy and happy, but I think it's important for them to learn to be responsible with their money. Stress and anxiety about money have had a big impact on us both and I want them to know how to handle it well when they feel the same stress someday. I read an awesome book by this really funny guy and I want to try some of the ideas. But I need your help to keep them accountable."

If they are the disengaged example, it could start like this: "We both love our kids and want them to be healthy and happy, and I think it's important for them to learn to be responsible with their money. Neither of us want them living in our basement and eating all our food when they're 35, so this will be a good way to get them started early. But I need your help to keep them accountable."

Inviting others to learn what you're learning is a great way to build a relationship and shared vision. I recognize it might be really awkward to read a book and discuss it weekly with an ex, but having them read the book, even if you don't have weekly discussions, will help create a shared vision and more common ground.

TALK ABOUT IT WITH YOUR CHILD

There will be some occasions where we want to talk with our children directly about the influence others—including media—are having on their finances. As you have probably noticed, there are countless apps, shows, channels, and platforms that promote an unhealthy desire for "stuff," specifically the particular stuff they are selling. The most direct way to address the situation is to limit their exposure to it.

For younger kids, this makes a lot of sense, but it has less of the desired impact as they get older. When Erica and I find that a YouTube channel or show promotes materialism in a way that is clearly unhealthy for our children, we shut it off. For the youngest kids, we just tell them the show is not good for them. For older kids, we give a little more explanation. For the oldest kids, we go into even greater detail about what the Bible teaches and how the show is teaching them the opposite.

With the older children we also want to incorporate objective criteria they can understand and apply in the future. Just saying, "This show isn't good for you," offers them truth about that show, but doesn't offer them criteria against which they can evaluate future shows. Consider expanding the explanation to, "This show isn't good for you. All they talk about is 'stuff.' They just want newer and better 'stuff.' God wants us to be content with what we have. If you're constantly seeing and hearing about how only more and better 'stuff' will make you happy, you're going to start believing it." This explanation helps them understand *why* you don't want them watching "shows about stuff." Rather than just giving them a specific instruction about a specific show, you've given them a set of criteria they can apply to future shows they watch.

When the negative financial influence is a person, it will usually be our kids who bring it up. "Well, Dave gets to . . ." or "Dave's parents take him to Dairy Queen every day and never make him buy his own ice cream!"

The first thing we want to do is be prepared for the conversation. Revisit the big-picture goal for handling your finances the way you do, the plan you've created to glorify God with your finances, and your commitment to prepare your kids to do the same. Reminding yourself of these will help you help them look at the situation from an eternally focused perspective.

Think ahead about how you will respond to their questions and objections. The conversation itself will train your children how to handle and resolve conflict, so think about (a) what behavior you want to model, (b) how you will explain the financial positions you've taken, (c) how you will explain the ground rules of conflict resolution, and (d) how you will give them practical opportunities to do the same.

Next, we want to be sure we don't undermine the other person's authority or insult their choices or way of life. We want to stick to our convictions and choices but avoid coloring the convictions and choices with our personal bias. I'm not advocating for a compromise of biblical principles, just limiting our appeal to the facts and *shared* assumptions.

For example, when that child asks, "Why do Dave's parents have really nice cars and a huge house and we have old cars and I have to share a room?" A biased and insulting response could be, "Because the Bible says we should be good stewards and having all that stuff is not being a good steward. That may not be important to Dave's family, but it's important to ours." The more effective and loving response could be, "The Bible teaches us to be good stewards of everything God gives us. God may want them to have those nice things, but He wants our family to give and save more instead of having those things." This doesn't compromise biblical truth, but neither does it insult them or undermine their authority to make decisions for their own family.

In a few circumstances, I've initiated the conversation after sensing that one of the kids really envied the lifestyle choices of friends or extended family members. I just open with, "It seems like you're really excited about all the nice stuff Dave's family has. I understand those things can seem exciting and their family sees value in them, but I want to explain why we choose to live like we do."

Again, none of this would be the first thing out of my mouth if I hadn't thought through the conversation ahead of time. Invest some time in preparing for these conversations before they come up, so you can be more thoughtful and accurate with your responses.

LIMIT EXPOSURE

Unfortunately, there will be times it is necessary to exercise control and limit your child's exposure to certain outside influences.

We see Paul instruct in 1 Corinthians 5:12-13, Ephesians 5:6-7, and Titus 3:10 the extreme measure of excluding members of the church from the community if they will not accept wise counsel and honor the community by doing what is right.

For influences like media and friends, this is somewhat straightforward to apply. With parents and family, not so much. For media, you may have to decide certain shows or channels aren't allowed. For friends, it may be allowing them to spend time together only in controlled environments. For example, if your child has a friend whose parents are consistently buying your child expensive things or including them in expensive activities, you may find them losing their humility and contentment and putting more value in "stuff" than they should.

Start by talking with your child and the friend's parents. If that doesn't have the desired impact, you may want to start inviting the friend over to your house or deciding your child can go over to the friend's house only once a month and to make sure they take their own spending money with them so they can pay for themselves (or at least offer to).

Again, we are called to be a *"kingdom and priests"* (Revelation 5:10) and a *"town on a hill"* (Matthew 5:14). Cutting off every non-Christian who lives differently than you isn't the answer. We should work to influence those around us and pull back only after we've found their influence to be detrimental and too strong for us and our kids to overcome at the time.

I would reserve limiting time with family members for only the most extreme circumstances, almost none of which relate to finances. In matters of neglect or abuse, be it mental, physical, financial, or otherwise, you will need to make some really tough choices. But in matters of abundance (aka spoiling), cutting someone off ends up making money seem *more* important than it is, adding to the problem. With family, the motivation behind excessive spending is almost always love. Talking to the family members about your goals will be a good start even if it doesn't fully resolve the issue.

DO YOUR BEST AND TRUST GOD

Unfortunately, there will be times when we have taken all the right steps but find ourselves unable to remove, or even limit, a negative influence in our children's lives. It is important to remind ourselves that God is chiefly concerned with our attitudes and actions (which are within our control), not the outcomes of those attitudes and actions (which exceed our control).

There will be people in your child's life who do not have the same goals, do not want to align with your plan, and do not want to support your choices, but who cannot be removed from your child's life. Continue following God's guidance. Continue to focus on the things you have control over (your own choices and actions). Continue to set a positive example for your children, and as often as you can, explain the whats and whys as you provide opportunities for them to engage. Continuing to love your children sometimes includes loving your enemy.

Our goal is perfection, but we do not control the outcome. God does. Our part is to be intentional in our efforts to teach and train our children: to provide Modeling, Verbal Instruction, and Practical Opportunities of godliness in our finances and every other area of our lives. Remember that doing something is infinitely better than doing nothing. Continue doing your part to the greatest extent you can and trust God to do His part to the extent that only He can.

GRANDPARENTS

Grandparents get their own section because they have greater influence than any other non-parent in our kids' lives. They are also among the most sensitive relationships of any of the outside influences.

Grandparents, from a kid's perspective, are the closest thing to superheroes they will ever know. They live secretive and unsuspecting lives and appear in times of extreme fun and crisis. They operate outside the normal rules and laws, offering relief from the monotonous day-to-day demands of Mom and Dad.

From the parents' perspective, grandparents are the most likely to ignore their requests and appeals—while offering unsolicited advice—but they are also among the group of "untouchables" because they offer so much good in the children's development. God tells us to honor our father and mother (Deuteronomy 5:16), offering no exceptions or limitations. It is by far one of the most precarious balances in parenting.

Please bear with me for a moment while I appear to digress into a different topic. You'll see shortly how this ties into our discussion of grandparents.

Having studied biblical financial principles for a long time and discovered my own idol to be retirement related, I believe there are three unique types of retirees in today's society, only one of which is biblical. The other two are my own observations, so while encouraging some healthy skepticism, I stand by them. I share them not to give you new labels for people but to help you better understand their way of thinking. The goal is to find common ground, build rapport, and get their support and help.

This should also be a topic of self-reflection for each of us to make sure we are working toward and planning for godly retirement.

The no-longer-working retiree. This person defines retirement as the absence of work. There is little-to-no plan of replacing work with anything in particular. They worked before, and now they don't, so they're "retired." Most of their time is spent doing basically nothing, with the occasional activity mixed in. For the record, this was my plan for retirement until God shut it down.

The no-rules-apply retiree. This person views retirement as a 20-30 year celebration of their hard work. Like a professional sports team whose intense discipline helped them win the championship, they're now spraying bottles of champagne with no sign of discipline to be found. They worked hard all those years so they could have freedom in their retirement, and they intend to cash in on it by doing whatever they want whenever they want.

The new-purpose retiree. This person views retirement as the opportunity to pursue their passions and be more focused on fulfilling their purpose without the distraction of having to earn a paycheck. They are more focused on what's ahead than what's behind. They see this stage in life as just as meaningful as their years of work, if not more.

As you could predict, this last one is the biblical one. The only time the Bible even alludes to "retirement" is when, in Numbers 8:23-25, it says:

> And the Lord spoke to Moses, saying, "This applies to the Levites: from twenty-five years old and upward they shall come to do duty in the service of the tent of meeting. And from the age of fifty years they shall withdraw from the duty of the service and serve no more" (ESV).

In this case, I have intentionally referenced the ESV rather than the NIV. While the ESV translates the stepping back from work as *"withdraw,"* the NIV uses the word *"retire."* I believe the NIV has done readers a disservice by overly modernizing the translation in this passage. "Retire" and "withdraw" are *denotative* synonyms since they have the same literal meaning, but the *connotative* definitions are very different since they evoke different emotional meanings. Most of us can hear the word "withdraw" without it being biased by any emotions. We recognize pretty cleanly that it means to step back or stop. "Retire," on the other hand, is too closely related to "retirement" in our culture, so we read our version of retirement *into* the text, rather than *out of* it.

What this passage teaches us is that the Levites, who were responsible for setting up, taking down, and maintaining the Tabernacle, were to withdraw from that work and transition into a mentoring role at the age of fifty. They were to stop being the ones doing the labor and start being the ones to train the next generation of laborers. They (and we) were never told to stop being productive, even though our roles and responsibilities change over time.

As I thought about the topic of a grandparent's role in influencing kids, I came to the conclusion that nearly every retired grandparent I knew grandparented the same way they retired. These are the corresponding grandparenting styles.

The no-longer-a-parent grandparent. This grandparent is no longer a parent of young children, and as with working, has little or no plan to intentionally influence their grandchildren. Seeing that as the parents' job, they will occasionally drop in but won't put much work into the endeavor. They see themselves as absent of any significant responsibility.

The no-rules-apply grandparent. This grandparent celebrates the notion that their time as a responsible parent is over. Now they can enjoy being a grandparent any way they want. Even if they parented in the past with strict and well-reasoned rules, this intentionality doesn't carry over to their role as grandparent. Rule enforcement is the parents' job and grandparents are just meant to be fun.

The new-purpose grandparent. This grandparent sees their role as distinctively different from that of a parent but as still endowed with specific and intentional purpose. They recognize their influence as borderline superheroes and leverage it to support both the parents' and the children's development.

As you could again predict, this last one is what the Bible calls grandparents to be and do. We hear a little more about the role of older Christians in Titus 2:2-5:

Teach the older men to be temperate, worthy of respect, self-controlled, and sound in faith, in love and in endurance.
Likewise, teach the older women to be reverent in the way they live, not to be slanderers or addicted to much wine, but to teach what is good. Then they can urge the younger women to love their husbands and children, to be self-controlled and pure, to be busy at home, to be kind, and to be subject to their husbands, so that no one will malign the word of God.

This chapter of Titus teaches us about the distinctive and complementary roles of young and old. While the parent is responsible for the protection, provision, and preparation of their children, they need the guidance, wisdom, and support of their own parents.

Parents should take the same approach with grandparents as with other outside influences, but with an extra measure of prayer, respect, honor, and love. Seek to understand their perspectives and motives. Find common ground to build from. Build rapport outside of any specific topics of dispute. Explain your position and invite them to help. Have them read and discuss this book with you. If they can align with the goals, the methods will be easier to agree on.

TO GRANDPARENTS

In preparing for this chapter, I had many fun and enlightening conversations with Compass team members on their approaches to the parenting/grandparenting relationship. The Compass team is largely made up of "New-Purpose Retirees," those who have left the professional arena and now spend their time focusing on helping others learn, apply, and multiply biblical financial principles.

We also have several team members, though, who are parents of younger children. Through one-on-one conversations and robust roundtable discussions, I've had the opportunity to hear about the good, bad, and ugly approaches on both sides: grandparents who have honored God, their kids, and their grandkids by thoughtful and intentional efforts; parents who have honored their fathers and mothers and their children in the same way. On the other hand, I've heard about grandparents who have made their children's parenting efforts more difficult—and parents who have not thought and prayed through their decisions and responses.

As I worked through my notes, I felt the best practices for "New-Purpose Grandparents" fit nicely into the two major categories below. The best practices for parents were consistent with the first 14.75 chapters of this book and won't be revisited here.

Continue leveraging your influence with your kids (the parents). Most parents are figuring it all out as they go. They talk with other parents, read books, and try to learn from their mistakes. They subscribe to blogs, listen to podcasts, and start support groups at their church. All the while, you're just a call away with decades of experience under your belt, both good and bad. Your experience and wisdom, offered in a non-threatening way, can further strengthen their relationships with you and their kids.

Offer ideas rather than suggestions or criticisms. Tell stories about your struggles and failures so they know they aren't alone. Follow these up with recollections of what worked for you. Support them in front of their children and talk to the parents later if they could have handled a situation better. If they aren't teaching their kids godly financial principles, invite *them* to take the lead with their kids rather than taking it upon yourself. Your kids still want and need your guidance, but in a way that doesn't feel like you're trying to control them.

Respect the parents' position and authority as parents. Use your near-superhero status to reinforce the love and authority of the parents. Your affirmation and support further solidify the parents' authority with their children. Even if you think they're doing it wrong, allow them to be the parents.

If you want to give your grandkids something significant or lots of insignificant things, ask their parents if it's okay and how they would like it to be handled. If you want to make an exception to a rule they have, talk to them about it first. This gives them the opportunity to think and pray about what's best for their family without feeling rushed or forced.

Remember what it was like to be in their position. Explain your goals and motives. They want you to have a great relationship with your grandkids, but it often takes days or weeks to put certain rules and routines, once broken, back into place.

There is a lot more instruction in Scripture on the responsibilities of a parent than a grandparent, and it is the parents who will be accountable for the way their children were raised. Just as you will be with yours. You will only be accountable for the way you *grandparented* their kids.

Encourage, challenge, and support your children to be the best, most God-glorifying parents they can be. God will honor your efforts, regardless of whether they follow your lead.

In many ways, biblical grandparenting is as much work as biblical parenting. Like the "retired" Levites whose roles became less essential to the daily functions of the tabernacle but more essential for the long-term sustainability of the community, your role as a grandparent is episodic but more diverse than that of a parent. While you get more breaks and time away from the watchful eyes of young children than someone who is actively parenting their in-home kids, you now have the opportunity to continue influencing your adult children as you enjoy the additional opportunity to influence your grandchildren. Your experiences and perspectives are invaluable to both, and your wisdom and influence will help create stability and faithfulness across multiple generations.

THREE BIGGEST TAKEAWAYS FROM THIS CHAPTER

1)

2)

3)

CHAPTER 15

MVP Everything

> *"You are the light of the world. A town built on a hill cannot be hidden. Neither do people light a lamp and put it under a bowl. Instead they put it on its stand, and it gives light to everyone in the house. In the same way, let your light shine before others, that they may see your good deeds and glorify your Father in heaven."*
>
> MATTHEW 5:14-16

So far, we have stayed pretty focused on the application of the MVP model to our families: (1) specifically our parenting, (2) more specifically to teaching our children what God says about money and possessions, and (3) even more specifically, how to help our children create and execute a budget that honors God with their finances.

One of the things I love about the MVP methodology is that it's not limited to budgeting, finances, parenting, or even our families at all. The model can be applied just as well to teach anything to anyone the way Jesus did. Here's a short list of suggestions and idea starters for how and where you can apply the MVP methodology inside and outside your home.

BEYOND OUR BUDGETS

Let's first expand a bit within the domains we've been developing: our families, our children, and their finances. We can apply the MVP model to things other than their budgets.

College Savings

Modeling. What does the Bible teach about saving for college, and how can I do it in a way that will engage my children?

As previously discussed, the Bible encourages us to practice *"steady plodding"* (the phrase comes from Proverbs 21:5, TLB) and to save for things in advance as soon as we know the expense is coming (Proverbs 21:20). It is wise to estimate the future cost of college by looking at historical costs and talking to our children about what sort of college they would want to go to and what they want to be when they grow up.

At age four, they want to be a unicorn or a monster truck, so no college may be necessary, but we can start saving a basic amount anyway in case they change their mind. When they're 16, they'll have a better idea of where they may want to go and what they may want to study. You can also begin to have the conversation that some colleges and courses of study may not be in scope because of financial limitations. Maybe they need to plan on attending a community college for the first two years or they will need to settle on a state school. It will be better to tell them Harvard isn't an option now than after they've been accepted.

Verbal Instruction. How can I explain what I'm doing in a way they can understand?

Once you have a plan for how much to save and for how long, you can explain to them your strategy and reasoning. Maybe you're going to put $250 per month into a 529 plan to get the tax benefits. If you start when they're four years old and assume six percent growth, you can show them how you will have $65,000 saved for them when they go to college at age 18. Maybe you can get better performance and growth by using something other than a 529 plan. Explain all of that to them at a level that is appropriate for their age.

More than the math, you want to focus on how saving over time adds up and that your goal is to give them the opportunity to reach their full potential and have the greatest impact for the kingdom.

Practical Opportunities. How can I give my child the opportunity to be part of the process?

Allowing them to be part of the planning and saving processes helps them understand the cost and value of a college education. Not many children are going to jump at the chance to save for their own education, but requiring them to contribute to some portion of the cost will give them valuable experience and perspective, as well as a financial stake in their education.

My parents paid for two years of college, but I was responsible for anything more. The result was me blowing my personal savings on a new truck and taking out loans to cover the last two years of college. This was probably not what they had in mind when they came up with the strategy, but I had to deal with the consequences of my decision and am better off because of the hard lesson learned.

Investing

Modeling. What does the Bible teach about financial investing, and how can I do it in a way that engages my children?

The Bible never addresses the stock market or any growth vehicles beyond cattle and crops, but it says a lot about the attitudes of our hearts when we invest. We're taught to invest for long-term gain (Proverbs 21:5), to seek wise counsel (Proverbs 20:18), to diversify (Ecclesiastes 11:2), and to avoid taking excessive and unnecessary risks (Ecclesiastes 5:13-14). We must first make sure we are investing wisely by God's judgment rather than our own.

Verbal Instruction. How can I explain what I'm doing in a way they can understand?

Telling your children about your investment strategies—the whats, hows, and whys—helps them understand how God's perspective determines your strategy. How much do you invest each month or year, and why? How do you handle college savings, retirement savings, and general savings differently, and why? What are the implications of more and less aggressive investment strategies, and why have you chosen some over others?

Practical Opportunities. How can I give my child the opportunity to be part of the process?

Whether it's a mock investment account for fun, their own custodial IRA or brokerage account, or just helping you choose investment options for your accounts, allowing children to practice wise investing with small amounts of money can build understanding and competence at an early age. You have the opportunity to help and influence, and the mistakes they make will be smaller than when they get their first 401(k) or an inheritance.

BEYOND OUR FINANCES

Moving outside our finances, we can and should teach and train our children to have godly attitudes and behaviors in everything they do.

Worshiping God

Modeling. What does the Bible teach about worshiping God, and how can I do it in a way that engages my children?

The Bible teaches that our worship of God should be Spirit-filled, unrestrained, and a top priority in our lives. The best example can be found in 2 Samuel 6. David celebrates the return of the Ark of the Covenant by singing and dancing to the Lord and isn't ashamed of it at all. His wife thinks he makes a fool of himself, but he is unwavering.

Our worship doesn't always have to include singing and dancing, but it should always be consistent with what the Spirit puts on our heart. If the Spirit says to dance, dance! If the Spirit says to sing, sing! If the Spirit says to confess, confess! We should always make being part of a local church a priority since God's word instructs us to (Hebrews 10:25). Proper worship of the King of kings is the greatest of life skills, but it starts with our commitment to provide modeling for our children.

Verbal Instruction. How can I explain what I'm doing in a way they can understand?

Once again, simply be open about the whats, hows, and whys of worship. Reading them the story of David worshiping God or Elisha and the prophets of Baal in 1 Kings 18 (one of my personal favorites) will get their attention. Then we can explain that when God said to worship, both men did exactly as the Spirit instructed.

Follow this up by relating it to the normal things we do to worship God. We go to church on Sundays to sing praises and learn more about Him. We pray to Him throughout the day and listen to songs about him. We commit everything we do to His honor and glory because He deserves it. We can't call fire down from heaven, but we can raise our voices, lift our hands, and move our feet!

Practical Opportunities. How can I give my child the opportunity to be part of the process?

Inviting our children to come with us to church, to sing with us in the car, and to pray with us throughout the day helps them be part of our life and build a relationship of their own with Jesus. Taking turns praying at meals or letting them pick the next Christian song on a road trip helps them take an active interest in worshiping God rather than passively accommodating their idea of force-fed monotonies like singing the same songs and listening to the same Pastor.

Personal Growth

Modeling. What does the Bible teach about personal growth, and how can I do it in a way that engages my children?

Each of us is called to continually grow in our knowledge and understanding of God's word (Psalm 119, 2 Timothy 3:16). We can model this for our children by reading the Bible every day as well as reading other books, watching videos, and discussing them with friends to gain new perspectives and understanding. Let your kids see you doing these things to help them realize that this is part of the Christian life.

Verbal Instruction. How can I explain what I'm doing in a way they can understand?

Explain to your children why continually enriching your knowledge and understanding of God is important. Tell them about how our different experiences and situations in life bring light to different truths in Scripture. Talk with them about how a particular verse had specific meaning to you in the past but now has another application in your new season of life.

Practical Opportunities. How can I give my child the opportunity to be part of the process?

Invite your children to continue learning what the Bible teaches. Help them get involved in Sunday School or a Small Group. Invite them to read a book or watch videos with you and discuss what you are learning. These things aren't time consuming or difficult, but they require commitment and persistence from both you and them.

Service

Modeling. What does the Bible teach about service, and how can I do it in a way that engages my children?

The Bible encourages us to serve anyone and everyone as often as we are able. It teaches us that if we humble ourselves before God and men, God will exalt us (1 Peter 5:6). It teaches us that the least on earth will be the greatest in heaven (Luke 9:48). We are to care for widows and orphans (James 1:27), which should be applied both literally to widows and orphans but also figuratively to any who are unable to care for themselves.

We should be active and intentional about serving others inside our homes, our communities, and anywhere else we interact. We should not only open doors for people and help them get their carts back to the corral at the grocery store but also make longer-term commitments to care for people in ways they can't care for themselves. Commit to mowing lawns for the elderly in the summer and shoveling snow for them in the winter. Commit to driving a person to and from work or church if they don't have a vehicle or are unable to drive themselves. Do it all with your kids watching.

Verbal Instruction. How can I explain what I'm doing in a way they can understand?

Explain to your children what God says about service and about the reward we get in heaven if we serve those who cannot repay us on earth (Luke 14:12-14). Allow them to ask questions, and give them honest answers. Maybe someone else *should* be mowing the person's lawn or shoveling their steps, but we have the opportunity to share Christ's love with them—so *we* will.

Practical Opportunities. How can I give my child the opportunity to be part of the process?

Invite them to help with your service, giving them meaningful but appropriate tasks. Their job may just be talking to the person or picking up sticks, but when they do it to the glory of God, He will honor and reward their contribution and they will learn the value of serving others.

BEYOND OUR KIDS

Moving outside of parenting, we can also influence others within our families using the MVP model. The MVP methodology always embraces influence over control, but with adults, we'll need to completely let go of control. These are grownups, and you have little or no authority over the choices they make, but you can still influence them. In this section, I will illustrate one example for each relationship type, but each could just as easily be applied to the other relationships.

Spouses

Modeling. How can I demonstrate an attitude or behavior I think is important to my family in a way that will engage my spouse?

If you want your spouse to start doing something, begin by doing it yourself. If, for example, you want to start budgeting, start by budgeting the money you have control over, and don't be secretive about it. Set aside time every week to work on your personal budget when you know they'll be around. Use envelopes and trackers so they can see that you're doing something new; this helps arouse curiosity.

Verbal Instruction. How can I explain what I'm doing in a way they can understand?

After you've established a consistent habit of budgeting, you can explain the what, how, and why in a way that's appropriate (not over- or under-explaining) and at a time when they are likely to listen. Engage your spouse in a conversation, asking them what they think about an idea and sharing your own opinions and perspectives. Invite them to read a Bible-based book on the topic together and discuss what each of you learned from each chapter.

Practical Opportunities. How can I give my spouse the opportunity to be part of the process?

Actually listen to hear, and incorporate their ideas. Allow them autonomy to do things the way they think they should be done. With children, we talked about being intentional with the opportunities we give them. We wanted to give them opportunities that were challenging enough to be engaging but not so challenging that they caused frustration or failure.

Although adults will generally have the ability to take on more challenging roles, we should use a similar approach as we do with our children. If we think God will be glorified by creating a monthly family budget, we want to avoid two common mistakes: (1) excluding our spouse, or (2) giving them technically challenging tasks (like writing nested "If" formulas or applying conditional formatting to a spreadsheet when they don't know how). Either of these encourages them to check out as quickly as our kids do.

Parents

Modeling. How can I demonstrate an attitude or behavior I think is important to my parents in a way that will engage them?

As with your spouse, if you want your parents to start doing something, begin by doing it yourself. If, for example, you want them to be more involved in church, start by making sure you are highly involved in church. Make this a priority in your life. Schedule family events and activities around those of the church and be willing to be a little late to things when they interfere with Sunday service. Attend church services when your family is out of town, even if you have to go alone.

Verbal Instruction. How can I explain what I'm doing in a way they can understand?

After you've established a consistent habit of making church a priority, you can explain the what, how, and why in a way that's appropriate (not over- or under-explaining) and at a time when they are likely to listen. Engage them in a conversation, asking them what they think about an idea that was presented in a recent service or sermon and sharing your own opinions and perspectives. Invite them to read a Bible-based book on a topic together and discuss what each of you learn from each chapter.

Practical Opportunities. How can I give them the opportunity to be part of the process?

Since they are grownups and probably have their own independent lives, the main practical opportunities will come by way of invitations. Invite them to church. Invite them to your Small Group. Invite them to serve alongside you. As they see and hear the impact your relationship with a local church has had in your life, they will be more open to giving it a try themselves. Help coordinate those opportunities. Go to the church they want to try out, even if it's not your home church or one you will particularly enjoy. Help them get involved in their own church community so that they can know the full depth of Christ's love and learn to share it with others.

Adult Children and Grandchildren (Remember, you're a borderline superhero, and with great power comes great responsibility.)

Modeling. How can I demonstrate an attitude or behavior I think is important to my adult children and grandchildren in a way that will engage them?

As with spouses and parents, if you want your adult children and grandchildren to start doing something, begin by doing it yourself. If, for example, you want the family to be more affectionate or encouraging with one another, start by being more affectionate and encouraging with them. Compliment them when they do something well. Console them when they try something and fail. Praise in public and correct in private, both in love.

Verbal Instruction. How can I explain what I'm doing in a way they can understand?

After you've established a consistent habit of encouraging and celebrating, you can explain the what, how, and why in a way that's appropriate (not over- or under-explaining) and at a time when they are likely to listen. Engage your adult children and grandchildren in a conversation, together or separately depending on the topic. Ask them what they think about an idea and share your own opinions and perspectives. Invite them to read age-appropriate, Bible-based books on the topic together and discuss what each of you learn from each chapter.

Practical Opportunities. How can I give them the opportunity to be part of the process?

Invite your adult children and grandchildren to encourage one another. "Jerry, did you see how Tommy balanced the stuffed bear on one foot?! Isn't that amazing?" Or, "Janice, did you hear that Janie got a B on her last math test? She said that was the hardest chapter of the year and the highest grade was only a B+. Isn't that great?"

Maybe even pull your adult child aside and tell them you want to celebrate by taking everyone out for ice cream but would like it to come from them, not you. These types of things reinforce the importance of encouraging and celebrating each other. Allowing the parent to be the hero makes them more likely to take the lead next time.

BEYOND OUR FAMILIES

Discipling others through the MVP approach is effective outside our families as well. By showing, telling, and allowing others to try, we can help anyone, anywhere learn new approaches and skills—whether in finances or other areas of our lives.

Friend, Employees, and Coworkers

The approach with friends, employees, and coworkers is similar to that with other adults, so I won't go through it again. Friends are a great mission field because we already have common interests, an established rapport, and opportunities to spend time together. By definition, friends are people we care about and know well, and who care about us and know us well. We are able to share with them our successes and failures more readily than with many others, knowing that they accept us with both. When something is going well in our life, they are likely to know it before we tell them, and they will often be quicker to notice changes in the way we approach things—sometimes even before our kids and spouse.

If there's something specific you want to share with a friend, think through how you can provide modeling, verbal instruction, and practical opportunities in a natural way. Tell them that you started budgeting to take them to lunch twice a month instead of once, and you'll pique their curiosity. Invite them to read a book on a topic you're both interested in or struggling with, and discuss what you're learning. Offer them full access to how you manage things in your life if they ever think it would be helpful.

In the workplace, the MVP methodology is consistent with ideal leadership principles and qualities. My favorite bosses and coworkers have always been the ones who could: (1) show me how to do something or navigate a specific situation, (2) tell me what was important and unimportant in the way they handled it, then (3) allow me to do it. Whether it was changing the band on a bandsaw or presenting to the Board, I wanted to see it done, hear why it was done that way, and then be given the opportunity to do it myself.

Developing junior members or investing in your peers will build them up, help them be successful, and make them more open to you sharing your other experiences and perspectives—like how a relationship with Jesus Christ changed your life or how learning and applying biblical financial principles has made your relationship with Him even stronger.

I know that these days people get fired for sharing their faith at work, but I believe it's usually because they haven't done the groundwork of developing a strong relationship before sharing their faith. When a coworker genuinely believes you care about them as a person because you've coached and mentored them, they are more likely to ask what you're always reading on your breaks and how your weekend was. And they are much less likely to report you to HR when you tell them you read the Bible on your breaks and your weekend was great because the church service Sunday morning was especially good.

I worked for eight years in a large company that did everything they could to keep God in the parking lot. I proudly displayed a cross on my desk, right next to my Bible. I helped junior members learn how to budget. I led a Bible study in the conference room during lunch breaks. There are two men whose names are now written in the Book of Life because of it, each committed to making disciples who make disciples.

I knew I might get fired, but I genuinely cared for my coworkers and employees and wanted to see them grow and develop as people. I followed the rules as they were written and intended, but I built strong relationships by showing my coworkers Christlike love and sharing the gospel every chance I had.

Compass-finances God's way's vision is to see everyone, everywhere faithfully living by God's financial principles in every area of their lives. Everyone, everywhere, in every area. While we've been called specifically to the area of money and possessions, it has always been with the goal of seeing those financial principles applied in every area of everyone's lives. Our battleground may be one of the wallet, but the war is one of the heart, and the stakes are those of eternity.

I pray that this brief examination of God's financial principles and application of Howard Dayton's MVP Parenting bears fruit in every area of your life. And the lives of your children—and their children—until the day our King returns.

THREE BIGGEST TAKEAWAYS FROM THIS CHAPTER

1)

2)

3)

Chapter 16

Finishing Well

Howard Dayton is the founder of Compass—finances God's way. He has written some closing thoughts on financial discipleship and finishing well.

When people used to ask evangelist Billy Graham how they could pray for him, he invariably responded, "Pray that I finish my life well and don't dishonor the Lord." He recognized how rare it was for people to remain faithful to the Lord, fully engaged in their calling to the end.

Can you imagine anything better than finishing well and having these words of Jesus ring in your ears throughout all eternity? *"Well done, good and faithful servant . . . enter into the joy of your master"* (Matthew 25:21, ESV).

It sounds wonderful, but it can be a challenge. Of the 2,930 people mentioned in the Bible, we know significant details of only one hundred. And of those one hundred, only about one-third finished well. Most of the other two-thirds failed in the second half of their lives.

Solomon is a classic example of someone who started out great but failed miserably later in life. Think about it: few people have started out as well and with more promise than Solomon.

- He was loved by God. *". . . The Lord loved [Solomon] and*

sent word through Nathan the prophet that they should name him Jedidiah (which means beloved of the Lord)" (2 Samuel 12:24-25, NLT).
- His father was King David, who authored most of the of Psalms and was described by God as *"a man after my own heart"* (Acts 13:22).
- Solomon made great choices early and was given more wisdom than any person. He wrote most of the book of Proverbs.

But then Solomon stopped following the Lord and descended into a life of disobedience. Deuteronomy 17 lists three things the kings of Israel were prohibited from doing.

- He must not acquire many horses for himself or cause the people to return to Egypt in order to acquire many horses.
- He shall not acquire many wives for himself, lest his heart turn away.
- He shall not acquire for himself excessive silver and gold.

So, what does Solomon do?

- He acquires twelve thousand horses imported from Egypt.
- He has seven hundred wives, and his wives lead him astray.
- He amasses silver and gold for himself.

He was completely disobedient to the Lord. And the consequences were disastrous for Solomon, his family, and for the entire nation of Israel. Clearly, starting well does not guarantee that a person will finish well.

In your journey with the Lord, it's not how you start that matters. It's how you finish. The Christian life is a marathon, not a hundred-meter sprint. Distance racing takes perseverance and determination, not speed. Distance runners need to pace themselves so that they finish the race—fixing their eyes on the prize and finishing well.

Paul illustrates this from his own experience. *". . . one thing I do:*

forgetting what lies behind and reaching forward to what lies ahead, I press on toward the goal for the prize of the upward call of God in Christ Jesus" (Philippians 3:13-14, NASB).

Finishing well doesn't mean finishing with a perfect record. But it does mean learning from our mistakes, getting back on course, and pursuing the Lord with our whole heart. We need to work hard at building the kingdom of God as long as we are able—regardless of past failures. In the many years of Compass, we've seen people really struggle to finish well, and we've seen people flourish. We've noticed that the strong finishers have several key characteristics in common.

BIBLE-BASED

"All Scripture is God-breathed and is useful for teaching, rebuking, correcting and training in righteousness, so that the servant of God may be thoroughly equipped for every good work" (2 Timothy 3:16-17). Let's take a closer look at how Scripture has the ability to fully equip us on our Finishing Well journey.

There is simply no healthy Christian life apart from God's word. In the Bible, God tells us about Himself, enabling us to learn His ways and will. Only in the Scriptures do we find how to live in a way that truly pleases God.

When Jesus asked people about their understanding of the Scriptures, He often began with the words, "Have you not read?" He assumed that those claiming to be the people of God would have read the word of God. Unfortunately, this just isn't the case. A survey found that only 18 percent of Christians read the Bible every day, and 23 percent never do. So let's look at some ways we can break these trends and consistently be in God's word.

First, find the time. Perhaps one of the main reasons Christians never read through the entire Bible is its sheer length—it's BIG! At first glance it can feel overwhelming. But do you realize that you can read the entire Bible in 71 hours? Audio recordings prove it. In no more than 15 minutes a day you can read through the Bible in a year's time.

Another great practice is to find a Bible-reading plan. It's no wonder that those who simply open the Bible randomly each day soon drop the practice. Fortunately, there are some great Bible-reading plans available to help you stay consistent. Some Bibles are designed specifically to guide you through completing them in a year.

Each time you read, look for one phrase or verse to meditate on. Take a few minutes to think deeply about it. This will change your life. The Lord commanded Joshua, *"This Book of the Law shall not depart from your mouth, but you shall meditate on it day and night, so that you may be careful to do according to all that is written in it; for then . . . you will achieve success"* (Joshua 1:8, NASB).

Now, you may be thinking, "That's great for Joshua, but I've got a business or a household to run! I can't think about the Bible all day long. I've got decisions to make. It just isn't practical."

Let me assure you that meditation is the most practical thing in the world. Joshua didn't just sit around all day thinking about the Scriptures. He had two million people to manage. He was as busy, if not busier, than you are. So how does a busy person meditate on the Bible? Simple—read through a portion, and when a verse is especially meaningful to you, write it down. Take it with you, review it, and think about it during the day.

Finally, find a Bible study. Most of us will be way more consistent if we become involved in a Bible study. We need the encouragement and accountability of a group. And one of the greatest benefits of a group is developing close relationships with others who are also seeking to know the Lord better.

CHRIST-CENTERED

God's word is incredibly important in helping people finish well, but so is being Christ-centered. Since this may not be a term you hear every day, let's dig a little deeper into what it really means. It's actually pretty simple: if Jesus is the Lord of your life, you're going to do what He tells you to do. That's what it means to be Christ-centered.

When people surrender to the Lordship of Jesus Christ, they are acknowledging God's ownership and giving up their personal rights. This kind of obedience is a common theme we see among those who finish well. So, let's explore what it takes to be Christ-centered.

Our desire at Compass is threefold: helping people experience financial faithfulness, drawing them closer to the Lord, and encouraging them to surrender themselves to God. This includes recognizing that God owns it all, just as Psalm 24:1 tells us: *"The earth is the Lord's, and everything in it."*

Being Christ-centered isn't something we do just once; it is something we should strive to do every day, hour, and minute of our lives. It's a constant in the lives of those who finish well, and although it sounds challenging, there are several things we can do to make it a constant in our finishing-well journey.

A key factor in being Christ-centered is allowing the Lord to direct our paths. God is the only one who knows the direction we should take in our lives. Just as Israel was guided in the wilderness by the cloud and fire, and the apostles responded to Jesus when He said, *"Follow me,"* we must constantly be sensitive to the direction of the Lord in our business, our relationships, our ministry, and our daily lives. And this applies not only to the big decisions we face but also our small everyday decisions as well.

Paul gives us a good example of being Christ-centered. *"For I resolved to know nothing while I was with you except Jesus Christ and him crucified. I came to you in weakness with great fear and trembling. My message and my preaching were not with wise and persuasive words, but with a demonstration of the Spirit's power, so that your faith might not rest on human wisdom, but on God's power"* (1 Corinthians 2:2-5).

There is a lot of noise in this world on how to make the best decisions, how to be successful, and how to be the best you. Christ-centered people cover their ears to drown out this noise. They don't trust in the clever things of the world, but rather, humbly depend upon Jesus Christ to guide and direct their steps.

A second important factor in being Christ-centered is fruitfulness. A Christ-centered person recognizes that the fruitfulness of their life is a direct result of their relationship with the Lord. John 15:1-5 tells us, *"I am the true vine, and my Father is the gardener . . . No branch can bear fruit by itself; it must remain in the vine. Neither* can you bear fruit unless you remain in me. I am the vine; you are the branches. If you remain in me and I in you, you will bear much fruit; apart from me you can do nothing." The more obedient and dependent we are on the Lord, the more fruitful we will be in our ability to love and serve others.

PRAYER-DRIVEN

James 1:5 tells us, *"If any of you lacks wisdom, you should ask God, who gives generously to all without finding fault, and it will be given to you."* Seeking the Lord's direction, provision, and protection through prayer must be a constant focus for us on our journey to finishing well. Prayer makes us more like Jesus as it shows us God's heart and reveals His wisdom. It is essential to us in understanding and doing His will.

If prayer could have been unnecessary for anyone, surely it would have been Jesus, the sinless Son of God. However, it was one of the dominant habits of His life and a frequent theme in His teaching.

> Mark 1:35 tells us that *"Very early in the morning, while it was still dark, Jesus got up, left the house and went off to a solitary place, where he prayed."*

> Luke 6:12-13 tells us that *"Jesus went out to a mountainside to pray, and spent the night praying to God. When morning came, he called his disciples to him and chose twelve of them, whom he also designated apostles."*

> And Luke 5:16 tells us, *"But Jesus often withdrew to lonely places and prayed."* This isn't something he did on occasion but was something that was a normal part of his life.

Sometimes Jesus got up early in the morning to pray, sometimes he spent the whole night praying, and sometimes he would just go off to a quiet place and pray. Regardless of when or where he prayed, it is clear that even in the demands of His public ministry, Jesus consistently spent time alone with His Heavenly Father.

Throughout the history of the church, those serving in leadership have recognized the importance of prayer. Samuel Chadwick said, "The one concern of the devil is to keep Christians from praying. He fears nothing from our prayerless work, prayerless religion. He laughs at our toil, he mocks our wisdom, but he trembles when we pray."

One of the most important factors in true intimacy with the Lord is honesty in our prayer life. As C. S. Lewis said, we should "lay before Him what is in us, not what ought to be in us." The Lord is thrilled that you are willing to come to Him as His child and spend time with Him, so come as naturally as you can. If you are hurting, share your pain. If you are confused, seek His guidance. If your joy is bubbling over, let it bubble over in praise. Being honest and transparent in your prayer time can take your prayer life and your relationship with the Lord to another level.

HOLY SPIRIT-LED

We cannot be truly Christ-centered, Bible-based, or Prayer-driven without being led by the Holy Spirit. Just as Jesus depended on the Holy Spirit to reveal the will of the Father to Him, we need to be completely dependent on Him to reveal God's will to us.

John 14:15-17 tells us, *"If you love me, keep my commands. And I will ask the Father, and he will give you another advocate to help you and be with you forever—the Spirit of truth. The world cannot accept him, because it neither sees him nor knows him. But you know him, for he lives with you and will be in you."*

When we translate the Greek word for advocate, we see that it refers to someone coming alongside somebody, someone who plays the role of an encourager and urges people on. Our advocate isn't just some random spirit floating around; the Holy Spirit has a home, and that home is you. He literally lives in those who love the Lord—every believer.

Of all the gifts given to us, none is greater than the presence of the Holy Spirit. So, let's take a closer look at some of the ways the Holy Spirit helps us on our journey of finishing well.

One of the many ways that the Holy Spirit helps us is through insight. Think of it this way: have you ever had a verse you had read years earlier suddenly come to mind—exactly when you needed it most? That's not luck, and it's not a coincidence. It's the Holy Spirit prompting you with God's provision for that moment.

John 14:26 tells us, *"But the Helper, the Holy Spirit, whom the Father will send in My name, He will teach you all things, and bring to your remembrance all that I said to you" (NASB).*

In addition to insight from the past, the Holy Spirit gives us insight into the present. As we are reading and studying Scripture, it is the Holy Spirit who teaches us, guides us, and helps us to understand the truth of God's word.

The Holy Spirit also teaches us to be more like Jesus. *"And we all, who with unveiled faces contemplate the Lord's glory, are being transformed into his image with ever-increasing glory, which comes from the Lord, who is the Spirit"* (2 Corinthians 3:18).

Although Moses got to experience God's glory on a mountaintop, the Holy Spirit gives us the opportunity to experience God's glory each and every day, no matter where we are!

Theologian Warren Wiersbe says it this way, "Moses reflected the glory of God, but you and I may radiate the glory of God. When we meditate on God's word and in it see God's Son, then the Spirit transforms us! We become more like the Lord Jesus Christ as we grow from glory to glory."

It is the Holy Spirit that equips us to be more like Christ, constantly transforming us and renewing us into His image.

And the Holy Spirit is also the giver of gifts—gifts given to believers that are essential to the proper functioning of the Church. No one receives all the gifts; they're uniquely dispensed to God's people according to His plan for each person.

"Now there are varieties of gifts, but the same Spirit; and there are varieties of service, but the same Lord; and there are varieties of activities, but it is the same God who empowers them all in everyone. To each is given the manifestation of the Spirit for the common good" (1 Corinthians 12:4-7, ESV).

These gifts are given to us to equip us for the calling God has put on our lives. They aren't meant to be put on the shelf for a later date; they are given to us for the here and now, and for a purpose.

So, I'd encourage you to think about how God is calling you and how you are using the gifts the Spirit has given you—for His glory.

DISCIPLESHIP-FOCUSED

Matthew 28:19-20 tells us, *"Therefore go and make disciples of all nations, baptizing them in the name of the Father and of the Son and of the Holy Spirit, and teaching them to obey everything I have commanded you. And surely I am with you always, to the very end of the age."*

The word "disciple" essentially means "learner." The Great Commission, the last instruction Jesus gave, reflects His personal priority and greatest investment of time: making disciples by teaching them how to obey everything He commanded.

Although Jesus taught the multitudes, He focused on the few. Jesus knew that making disciples was crucial for succeeding generations to follow. The same Holy Spirit gives each member of the body different gifts, but all of us are commanded to make disciples.

A big part of the Finishing Well journey is being discipleship-focused. This means examining how we are personally growing as disciples and also how we are making disciples by pouring our lives into others. So, let's explore some ways we can be discipleship-focused.

One of the main characteristics of disciples is that they strive to imitate Jesus. Luke 6:40 tells us that *"A disciple is not above his teacher, but everyone when he is fully trained will be like his teacher"* (ESV).

When it comes to discipleship, the goal is to imitate the life of Christ. And in order to help believers grow as disciples, we must be willing not only to tell them how but also to show them how. Paul said, *"Be imitators of me, as I am of Christ"* (1 Corinthians 11:1, ESV). And in Philippians 4:9 he wrote, *"What you have learned and received and heard and seen in me—practice these things, and the God of peace will be with you"* (ESV). He not only gave verbal instructions to the believers, he also lived out his faith before them.

Another key characteristic of disciples is that they bear fruit. Let's look at what Jesus says in John 15:5. *"I am the vine; you are the branches. Whoever abides in me and I in him, he it is that bears much fruit, for apart from me you can do nothing"* (ESV).

As we grow in our discipleship journey, we should start producing fruit, the fruit of the Spirit: love, joy, peace, patience, kindness, goodness, faithfulness, gentleness, and self-control. This doesn't mean we have to be perfect in all of these areas, but it does mean that the fruit of the Spirit will become more apparent in our lives as we grow on our discipleship journey.

Multiplication is the goal when it comes to discipleship. Disciples make other disciples: they replicate themselves; they reproduce. They desire to see lives transformed and see people grow in their relationship with the Lord.

Jesus focused on growing His disciples, but He had a greater end in mind: He wanted them to reproduce themselves. In the Great Commission, Jesus passes the baton to them, telling them to go and make disciples of all the nations.

Disciples aren't supposed to just sit on what they've learned: they are commanded to share the gospel with others and teach believers to be imitators of Christ. Disciples go after people with God's love, sharing Jesus with them. They also pursue other believers, mentoring and encouraging them in their faith. Inevitably, a person who is finishing well is someone who is walking alongside others on their discipleship journey.

CLOSING

Thank you for spending this time with us. In closing, I'd like to leave you with a few thoughts that have been powerful motivators for me.

Nothing on this planet comes close to knowing Jesus Christ and living a life that pleases Him.

- Leave your mistakes behind.
- Be courageous.
- Stay focused on Christ.
- Never give up.

Jesus finished well when He said, *"I have brought you glory on earth by finishing the work you gave me to do"* (John 17:4).

Paul finished well when he said, *"I have fought the good fight, I have finished the course, I have kept the faith"* (2 Timothy 4:7, NASB).

Our prayer is that you will finish well, too. That you will complete the task the Lord has given you so that you will hear these words ring in your ears throughout eternity: *"Well done, good and faithful servant . . . enter into the joy of your master"* (Matthew 25:21, ESV).

Howard Dayton

Howard Dayton, Founder, Compass—finances God's way

THREE BIGGEST TAKEAWAYS FROM THIS CHAPTER

1)

2)

3)

The *Compass - finances God's way*™
Vision, Mission & Values

Our Vision
To see everyone, everywhere faithfully living by God's financial principles in every area of their lives.

Our Mission
Equipping people worldwide to faithfully apply God's financial principles so they may know Christ more intimately, be free to serve Him and help fund the Great Commission.

Core Values

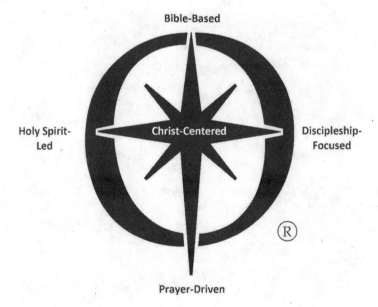

Continue the Journey...

Congratulations on completing Financial Discipleship for Families. We hope the Lord has had a significant impact on your financial discipleship journey through this book.

The financial discipleship journey is one that doesn't end until we hear the words *"well done, good and faithful servant."* We encourage you to continue this journey in one of two ways.

Continue your journey by engaging in studies, tools, and resources that will help you grow. Visit us at **ContinueGrowing.org** to learn more.

Continue your journey by paying it forward and helping others grow. To learn more, visit us at **HelpOthersGrow.org**.

Thank you for the time and effort you have invested in this book. We pray the Lord will draw you even nearer to Him as you continue to grow and help others grow.

About the Author

Brian Holtz was raised "going to church," but walked away from God in his teenage years. God called him back in his mid-20s around the time he met Erica, who had a similar story.

Married in 2007, they lived like most Americans do, not extravagantly but not intentionally. In 2010, also like many Americans, the financial crisis led Brian and Erica, along with their newborn son, to turn in desperation to God for financial help and guidance. He provided for them then and has continued to ever since.

Brian and Erica, along with their four children (Weston, Barrett, Rowan, and Eden), have learned to faithfully apply God's principles to their lives and are passionate about helping others do the same.

In his role as Chief Operating Officer at Compass-finances God's way, Brian applies learnings from his 15 years of cross-functional corporate experience to ensure the most efficient and effective use of the resources God has provided. In addition to his role at Compass, Brian also serves as an Elder and Lay Pastor at First Baptist Church in Muscatine, Iowa.

Endnotes

[1] Timothy Keller with Kathy Keller, *The Meaning of Marriage*, Penguin Books, 2016.

[2] R. Kent Hughes, *Disciplines of a Godly Man*, Crossway Publishing, 2019.

[3] Matthew Dixon, Nick Toman, and Rick LeLisi, *The Effortless Experience*, The Penguin Group, 2013.

[4] Howard Dayton, *Your Money Counts*, Compass-finances God's way, 2020.

[5] Robert E. Coleman, *The Master Plan of Evangelism*, Revell, 1993.

[6] BibleProject, *Proverbs*, https://bibleproject.com/explore/video/proverbs/

[7] Skye Jethani, *What if Jesus Was Serious?*, Moody Publishers, 2020.

[8] Cory Carlson, *Win at Home First*, Cloud Rider Publishing, 2019.

[9] Jerry Bridges, *Trusting God*, NavPress, 2008.

[10] Greg Gilbert, *What is the Gospel?*, Crossway, 2010.

[11] John Rinehart, *Gospel Patrons*, Reclaimed Publishing, 2013.

[12] Though not directly taken from this book, the inspiration for several of these ideas came about while reading Jesse Mecham, *You Need a Budget*, Harper Business, 2017.

[13] Jerry Bridges, *The Pursuit of Holiness*, NavPress, 2006.

[14] Though not directly taken from this book, many of the concepts in this section come from what I learned reading The Arbinger Institute, *The Outward Mindset*, Berrett-Koehler Publishers, 2016.